THE
LEADERSHIP EXPERIENCE

From Individual Success to
Organization Significance

RON CROSSLAND & GREGG THOMPSON

The Leadership Experience:
From Individual Success to Organization Significance

©2007 Ron Crossland and Gregg Thompson

This edition published by SelectBooks, Inc. For information address SelectBooks, Inc., One Union Square West, New York, New York 10003

First Edition

ISBN 978-1-59079-122-6

Library of Congress Cataloging-in-Publication Data

Crossland, Ron.
The leadership experience: from individual success to organizational significance / Ron Crossland and Gregg Thompson. -- 1st ed.
p. cm.
Includes bibliographical references and index.
ISBN 978-1-59079-122-6 (hardbound: alk. paper)
1. Leadership. I. Thompson, Gregg, 1950- II. Title.

HD57.7.C7655 2007
658.4'092--dc22

2007022974

Manufactured in the United States of America

10 9 8 7 6 5 4 3 2 1

from Ron

TO MY WIFE, SUSAN CROSSLAND,

WHO WAS BOTH AN INVALUABLE READER

AND LOVING FAN OF THIS WORK

from Gregg

IN MEMORY OF MY FATHER, RUBEN THOMPSON,

WHO GRACIOUSLY AND TIRELESSLY SPENT HIS LIFE

LABORING IN SERVICE OF HIS FAMILY

AND HIS COMMUNITY

Complimentary Online 360 Assessment

Each reader of The Leadership Experience is entitled to receive a personalized Leadership Experience Assessment (LEA) report. The LEA is an online assessment designed to provide you with confidential feedback on your leadership practices and potential from a group of individuals whom you select. The assessment contains forty behavioral statements using a standard one-to-five scale, and up to fifteen different observers can be invited to provide feedback for you. The LEA is designed to provide you with positive, constructive information that you will probably never receive elsewhere. The ratings and commentary contained in the LEA can greatly influence your development as a coach and as a leader. We strongly encourage you to take advantage of this opportunity.

To initiate the LEA process, simply go to:
www.theleadershipexperiencebook.com/lea
and enter the following code#: ELACH

Once your report is complete, it will be sent to you via e-mail.

Contents

We thank our fellow Bluepoint colleagues for their encouragement and support in the completion of this work. Kenzi Sugihara, a both wise and patient publisher, deserves more thanks than ink on a page can convey. We also thank Lynn Slavenski and Dave Faulk for reading and providing insightful comments on earlier manuscript drafts.

Preface

WE have spent the past twenty years working with thousands of leaders from the boiler room to the boardroom. We have worked as senior managers for large companies, and as entrepreneurs we have successfully been involved in several consulting and technology businesses. We have not only helped countless leaders grapple with the dilemmas and vagaries that leading presents, but have also experienced the demands of leadership firsthand. The net result of our experience is both simple and confounding: leading organizations is getting harder, not easier, to do.

We are students of leadership. Our particular point of view is the result of direct experience, advanced education, ongoing research, and a dedicated review of scholarly investigation and popular writing on leadership. We have developed our approach by forging what can be explained by theory, established by experiment, and experienced in the field. Our singular goal is ambitious: *we strive to better understand leadership, with all of its peculiarities, and use this knowledge to help accelerate the development of individual and organizational leaders everywhere.* Our work is sustained by our belief that:

- *Leaders make a difference.*

- *There is a growing undersupply of future leaders.*

- *Organizations increase their chances for renewal with more and better leaders.*

The leaders we work with, as well as the organizations we assist in developing leaders, are asking consistent, often unanswerable questions that especially haunt senior leaders:

- *What do I need to do to get employees fully engaged in this organization?*

- *How do I retain my free-agent-minded employees?*

- *How do I deal with snarling technologies that both advance and ensnare our organization?*

- *How do I deal with the growing multicultural problems we face in a world that oscillates between globalism and nationalism?*

- *How do we navigate the increasingly complex problems of shifting political realities in the various countries where we do business?*

- *Why is it that my personal actions seem to cause as much consternation as inspiration? Why do they seem to dissipate so quickly whether they are good or bad?*

- *How do I get more leadership going throughout my organization?*

- *Why do I feel as if I am becoming less relevant; how can I add more value?*

- *How do I stay the course of my convictions when results seem to be the sole measurement of success?*

- *How do I choose between managing my career and building a company that I will be proud of long after I leave, even if I am not remembered by subsequent generations?*

- *How do I satisfy voracious investors and disgruntled employees while keeping an eye on regulatory and environmental issues?*

- *What magic must I muster to create a sweeping innovative posture while dealing with increasingly difficult economic restrictions?*

- *Where do I find time to worry about people when economics and execution require all of my attention?*

- *Do I honestly want to lead, or do I simply want to make a lot of money for myself?*

IF you are reading this book, it's likely that several of these questions already strike a chord in your mind. And we would imagine you are saying to yourself, "These are really good questions and I would add this one ...." Leadership questions are endless, which is one reason that leadership study also seems endless.

This book may help you answer some of these questions. It takes questions of personal, individual leadership and questions of systemic, organizational leadership and integrates them into one straightforward model. Our thesis is that today's flattened, porous, networked, multicultural organizations demand that greater numbers of leaders at all levels understand how to be both individual leaders and organizational leaders. Furthermore, the tensions that exist between being an individual leader and an organizational leader are so difficult that organizations are experiencing a chronic shortage of people who either aspire to or can rise to the task of organizational leadership. Many leaders therefore focus strictly on their individual success as a leader, which provides considerable contribution on a temporary basis. However, this leadership doesn't provide the contributions needed to create effective, sustainable organizations.

There are two reasons why this development crisis occurs. First, too many leadership development efforts attempt to stretch individual leadership models beyond their limits to encompass organizational leadership issues. Second, too many organizational leadership development efforts focus on strategy, strategic thinking, or organizational design issues alone. And often they do not link these organizational leadership capabilities to individual leadership theory. Developing individual leadership capacity alone is a poor remedy for organizational leadership issues, and focusing on organizational leadership capabilities alone does little to remind managers of their individual leadership responsibilities. We see some leaders develop huge capacity in one or the other domain—individual or organizational leadership. It is rare to see a leader master both.

The Leadership Experience attempts to unify these two domains of leadership by considering how four timeless labors bind them together, as well as describe the tensions between individual and organizational leadership. We believe this model will help accelerate the possibility that greater numbers of future leaders will be able to unify their individual and organizational leadership abilities.

Should I Read This Book?

WE wrote this book for those of you who are attempting to answer the questions we have listed above and others like them. Although most of the examples we cite are business oriented, the leadership model we propose applies to any kind of organization. Whether you are struggling with how to handle the personalities and goals of a local community volunteer organization, venturing into a start-up company, devoting yourself to a political or religious calling, or ensuring the survival of a global business, the leadership model we propose may provide you with perspective for your situation.

The essence of this book is to provide a way of thinking about how a leader can extend his or her individual leadership success to the less visible perhaps but more important role of helping organizations achieve significance. There is little mystery left to questions of individual leadership, but many conundrums exist as to blending personal leadership skills with organizational leadership needs. We believe that those of you who are grappling with how to leave your organization in better shape than you found it, who aspire not just to making a personal mark in the world, but also to providing a healthy, inviting organization that attracts others to its cause, will be stimulated by our unique way of looking at leadership.

Notes

WE would particularly like to direct your attention to our use of the notes section at the end of the book. Not only have we cited our sources for your further exploration, but we have also included additional information about a variety of subjects for those who want to explore central ideas or a case study in more depth. You may also find interesting tangents, asides, and rambles that may prickle your senses, resulting in some delight if not insight. Regardless of the approach you choose, we thank you for allowing us to share our thoughts with you.

1 *The Four Labors of Leaders*

IN 2005, at the beginning of a yearlong leadership development process at BellSouth (now AT&T), Ron Frieson, president of the company's Georgia operations, attended the opening session to give a short talk and engage in some candid dialogue. Frieson is a dynamic, eloquent, and experienced executive, and his opening comments commemorate the fact that the participants have just crossed an important, often intangible, line of leadership responsibility: "For years during your career, you have often wondered what in the world was going on and at times you have simply scratched your heads, made a vague gesture upward, and remarked, 'I hope they know what they are doing.' Today you can no longer enjoy this privilege, for you have become they."[1]

Frieson's admonition that these experienced managers have entered into some of the highest levels of management responsibility and must now serve in a much more organizational leadership role than they ever have is delivered in an upbeat but serious manner. He emphasizes the fact that the boundary they have crossed has placed them in the hot seat of the "they," and that as senior organizational leaders, their perspectives will never be the same.

This passage from individual leader to organizational leader—from "this is my group" to "this is the corporation, city, nation, foundation, school, unit, ideology, or way of life I have chosen to lead"—doesn't just occur at some final rung on the hierarchical climb. The tension between individual and organizational leadership exists to some degree at *all* levels of leadership responsibility. And this tension creates both a barrier and an opportunity for individual leaders to integrate their individual, personal leadership abilities with their organizational or systemic leadership abilities. This book addresses what is involved in increasing the scope of leadership responsibility and integrating various levels of leadership demands as responsibility increases.

1

Leadership ability is abundant, but its perfection is rare. Nearly every person has led something at some time. We know because whenever we ask participants of any group to describe any significant leadership periods they've experienced over the course of their lives, they seem to easily and quickly recount them.

Episodic, temporary, project-oriented leadership has never been difficult to observe. Acting as an individual leader is very common, and the lessons from these episodes have a striking degree of similarity. Organizational leadership, however, is more difficult to observe and has far fewer examples. Although both oral and written histories have heralded the great deeds of organizational leaders, generally the emphasis in these stories has been upon the individual. From the agricultural aristocracy of the Sumer delta to the technologically adept of Silicon Valley, humans have strained to sift the notions of organizational leadership from the deeds of the individual leader. Leaders of Sumerian theocratic city-states used the word *lugal* as their term for king. Some *lugals* enjoyed kingship for the sake of having personal power. Some had as their major concern the general welfare of the city-state. During the twenty-fourth century B.C.E., near the end of the Old Sumerian period, a man by the name of Urukagina declared himself *lugal* of Lagash "and ended the rule of priests and 'powerful men,' each of whom, he claimed, was guilty of acting 'for his own benefit.'"[2]

Urukagina enacted laws concerning usury, theft, property disputes, and murder. He encouraged many freedoms that were unknown before his consolidation, such as supporting widows and orphans, and sought to ensure a positive future for all who lived in his lands. Some historians suggest that his code in particular supported women's issues to a greater degree than did the later, more famous codes of Hammurabi, Lipit Ishtar, or others associated with Assyrian or Babylonian governments.

Under Urukagina's rule, Lagash was prosperous and thus became an appealing takeover target. Eventually, Lagash was annexed by Lugal-Zage-Si, who consolidated it into his own lands to create a Sumerian empire. Sargon I, a Semitic ruler from Akkad, an ancient city located roughly halfway between Baghdad and Fallujah, conquered this Sumerian empire along with those operating out of Ur and Umman. Historians suggest that Sargon I was the first leader to consolidate a multiethnic society or empire. Records indicate that he "did not sleep in his efforts to promote prosperity and that in this new free enterprise economy trade moved as freely 'as the Tigris where it flows into the sea, ... all lands lie in peace, their inhabitants prosperous and contented.'" Text evidence suggests that Urukagina and Sargon I were admired both as individual or personal leaders and for the quality of their organizational leadership skills. Political scientists might consider them as being effective statesmen, not just beloved, or perhaps feared, politicians.

The reforms initiated by these two leaders helped promote a prosperous society—one that invented the potter's wheel and used wheel technology in several applications. In addition, Sumerian cuneiform was used largely by these political leaders to maintain an accurate commercial accounting and appears to predate Egyptian hieroglyphics. These societies engaged in astronomy, and their division of time into sixty-minute and sixty-second periods is still in use today. They grew Emmer wheat and barley with sophistication for their age, and were perhaps the first Asians to raise sheep and cattle on a grand scale.

The organizational concerns of these early leaders are echoed by leaders at financial services giant Wells Fargo. Wells Fargo isn't just concerned about financial success, but the company also strives to be a premier provider of services and one of the great places to work in America. Financial results, customer focus, and engaging a workforce might constitute a triple crown of visionary appeal in this modern age, but CEO Richard Kovacevich doesn't allow this sound bite to be swallowed without inspiring amplification. On the company's Web site he clarifies and imbues each point of the corporate vision with distinctive ideas; for example: "We'll promote the economic advancement of everyone in our communities, including those not yet able to be economically self-sufficient, who have yet to share fully in the prosperity of our extraordinary country. We'll be known as an active community leader in economic development, in services that promote economic self-sufficiency, education, social services and the arts."[3]

Another executive who is driven by the ideals of creating a great workplace and a workplace that gives back to the community is

Cisco CEO John Chambers. Since its inception, and despite its difficulties over time, Cisco has made significant contributions to the community. The company's vision includes statements about the future welfare of workers, companies, and countries. Chambers declares, "I truly believe that the Internet and education are the two great equalizers in life, leveling the playing field for people, companies, and countries worldwide. By providing greater access to educational opportunities through the Internet, students are able to learn more. Workers have greater access to e-learning opportunities to enhance and increase their skills. And companies and schools can decrease costs by utilizing technology for greater productivity."[4]

In an interview with *BusinessWeek*'s computer editor, Peter Barrows, Chambers related how giving back creates a reputation that precedes growth: "I know that has helped us in terms of international expansion. One top government official told me that 'one of the reasons you'll be successful here is that you give something back.'"[5]

These brief examples shed light on a repeated historical reality: lasting leadership is experienced not just by the individual leadership efforts of a great person, but also by the lasting impact of the organizational system that is created through organizational leadership efforts. Studying the personalities of Sargon I, Qin Shi Huangdi, Julius Caesar, Charlemagne, Elizabeth I, Catherine the Great, George Washington, and other famous leaders, it's easy to see that it is not simply their personal leadership abilities that immortalizes them, but also their organizational leadership legacies. From athletics to art, music to medicine, education to e-commerce, or performance arts to politics, there are many people who aspire to and achieve varying levels of excellence. In terms of personal leadership, most of these people make a contribution. Many of them make a difference in organizational ability. But fewer make a difference in *both* arenas. So although the qualities of personal leadership seem to be abundant, we suggest that sustained organizational leadership is somewhat rarer and more difficult to attain.

Defining, explaining, measuring, and understanding leadership has consumed decades of time, generated millions of data points, spawned a glut of theories, and created an industry of leadership development. Over the past ten years, however, it seems that repeated inquiries into what leadership is and how leaders lead has resulted in mere rumination. The competencies of leadership are no longer arcane mysteries to be explored. Each time we excavate this territory, we find the same basic story recast in a local dialect.

We have asked hundreds of experienced leaders to draw a schematic, diagram, or model of their personal leadership view. The results we have seen confirm this hypothesis: nearly everyone has learned a remarkably similar model of leadership. We believe the reason for this is that most of the leadership training, writing, and development in the world matches most people's personal experience of leadership. In fact, most leadership models are based upon observed leadership behavior. Therefore, modern corporate managers have created a sort of collective general understanding of what leadership is and what leaders do. However, there is not much new in leadership research. Any new study simply confirms what we already know or amplifies one particular aspect of leadership ability, such as vision, strategy, engagement, emotional maturity, presence, or any other popular leadership dimension.

One subject of ongoing research on leadership that particularly piques interest and controversy involves genetics. The jury is still out, and may remain out for some time, but serious researchers are not ignoring the data pouring in from the field of genetic/environmental interactions. For decades the idea of genetic predisposition easily tripped the "social Darwinism" reflex. Today most fully informed researchers have abandoned the nature-versus-nurture reasoning and have replaced it with one that considers the cooperative, dynamic interaction of environment *and* genetic operations. Some have altered the debate from nature *versus* nurture to nature *via* nurture. Others are skirting the schism created by a nature/nurture dichotomy and are attempting to look at the question through an adaptive systems view. Our understanding of how biological and environmental factors affect one another is increasing, and in the future we may be able to more fully understand how the constant lifetime interaction of a variety of experiences and the flexibility of genes to prepare and respond to these experiences shed light upon all components of the human condition, including leadership abilities.

If you review the content of the major models or theoretical descriptions of leadership, and then compare them with the extensive catalog of leadership research and cast an inquiring eye over the history of leadership, a remarkable but understandable pattern emerges: regardless of culture, epoch, or practitioner, there seem to be four unchanging, timeless labors that leaders encounter and engage. These four labors constitute an enduring meta-model of leadership, a model that acts as a structure for examining most of the hard-won research evidence on leadership. We use this meta-model to trace and present the four most consistent properties of the models we have observed, the most consistently studied and verifiable leadership components reviewed in scholarly literature, and the testing of this model with other learned leadership practitioners. This model will also serve to reveal the tensions between individual and organizational leadership that beleaguer and test modern leaders.

To place this model in context, however, we provide an overview of the evolution of leadership thought and research over the past century. Showing how leadership research has evolved allows us to focus this wide dispersion of light into a high-intensity beam of understanding about a subject that has already been studied to death yet continues to enthrall.

Leadership Science

LEADERSHIP science has a fascinating history, full of eccentric researchers, noble experiments, unexpected results, serendipitous events, superbly and poorly constructed theories, and contrary views. From personality or character trait theories to humanistic, psychoanalytic, or behavioral approaches, most research from 1920 to the 1970s revolved around personal theories of leadership. Most of the research concerned the person in the most senior leadership role or individuals of renowned stature—the great leaders. During this time, which we call the *transactional* period of leadership, the typical organization had a hierarchical structure. Increasing production was the primary organizational goal, and leadership was studied in terms of personal traits and the exchanges between leader and follower.

In 1978 James MacGregor Burns, a historian and a student of political science and leadership, popularized a phrase in his Pulitzer Prize–winning volume, *Leadership*, that labeled the direction of leadership inquiry: "Such leadership occurs when one or more persons engage with others in such a way that leaders and followers raise one another to higher levels of motivation and morality. Their purposes, which might have started out as separate but related, as in the case of transactional leadership, become fused ... thus it has a transforming effect on both."[6] *Transformational* leadership became the hottest word in the leadership lexicon, and this passage was one of the most frequently quoted from Burns's work.

The transformational leadership era focused on the deeper meaning of leadership or the transforming effects between leader and follower when they work toward mutually inspiring goals. This era began to look at the leadership-at-all-levels phenomenon and concluded that leadership episodes, or leadership actions, were abundant and cumulative. The period also saw a change in organizational structure from hierarchy to matrix. Leadership research focused on competencies (behaviors) rather than traits (personal characteristics), and the leading issue was empowerment rather than exchanges. Concerns about quality eclipsed those of production as the supreme organizational competitive advantage. This combination of factors dominated the minds of leaders and became both the melody and harmony lines for those composing leadership development scores.

Since the late 1990s, however, the rise of globalization turned the business world's attention to the complexities of global leadership. Leaders of multinational, and even local, companies became attentive to the effects of globalization, and a shift in emphasis occurred. The concept of engaging workers transcended the idea of merely empowering them as the key organizational issue. Matrix organizations gave way to the idea of networked organizations as work increasingly became dispersed over multiple time zones and cultures. Quality had erected a new barrier to entry into business, but these issues were by and large tamed to a degree that no longer allowed quality alone to provide advantage. Today, having achieved a sufficient level of parity between production and quality, the most promising competitive arena is *distinction*. Distinction is sought through design, innovation, brand loyalty, and other means.

Along with this new focus on distinction, a significant shift has occurred in leadership science. Research has moved from *understanding leadership* to *developing leaders*. The current period of leadership is what we call *transcultural*. There are abundant terms used to describe the phenomenon of a flattening world, including "globalism," "multiculturalism," "cultural diversity," "thinking global, acting local," and "ethnoconvergence." The macrosocial forces of educational, political, and commercial activity combined with the forces of rapid and prolific transportation and information technology (IT) are primary drivers of this cultural convergence.

Although driven by macrosocial forces, however, it's not just diversity or multiculturalism that is fueling this transcultural phenomenon. In the commercial world it is the sudden impact of hundreds and thousands of managers who are managing across cultural boundaries, an eruption of a need for global leadership talent that should have been anticipated but was not. Large-scale forces may be driving convergence, but the experience of convergence occurs at the individual level. For centuries, commerce has been a conduit that enables these global changes to be experienced locally.

Modern project-level leaders, as well as senior managers, deal with porous boundaries between multiple superiors and constituencies, teams and customers that form and reform in ever more fluid combinations, multiple time-zone issues that challenge our use of modern technology, and cultural concerns of infinite variety. Because of this, creating a brand-savvy, networked organization of highly engaged contributors yields a mind-bending difficulty that occupies a central place in senior leadership's attention.

The following table (Table 1) indicates the major shifts that have occurred over the past century in terms of leadership issues, research focus, organizational issues and structures, and the dominating strategic focus. During the transactional and transformational periods, leadership development as a discipline was practiced, although the variation among organizations was high. Much of the developmental emphasis focused on either exposing "movers and shakers" to various parts of an enterprise's operations and noting who did the best, or relying too much upon one key, experienced person who dominated the organizational culture. The later part of the transformational era did incorporate partnering with various educational institutions for rigorous study, known quaintly and unfortunately as sending high potentials off to "charm school." This era also saw the rise of executive MBA programs as de facto substitutes for effective leadership development.

	Transactional 1910 - 1978	Transformational 1978 - 1998	Transcultural 1998 - Present
Leadership Issue	Individual at the top	Individual at all levels	Global leaders
Research Focus	Traits	Competencies	Development
Organizational Issue	Exchanges	Empowerment	Engagement
Organizational Structure	Hierarchy	Matrix	Network
Strategic Focus	Production	Quality	Distinction

Table 1

At that time, identifying individual leadership competencies was the foreword to, not the book on, leadership development. Contemporary research has shifted to understanding how to effectively develop leaders and to questions of organizational leadership. As organizational systems have grown in complexity and reach, the idea that one person's actions and behaviors can account for all the causal variables of an organization's success or failure simply doesn't seem reasonable, if it ever did. Yet our individual and often collective knee-jerk analyses lead us to single out one person who is the mover and shaker in an organization, the primary actor who makes things stop or go. When the economy is going well, we want to applaud the president's, prime minister's, or monarch's prescience. When we lose our job, we want to blame the CEO's incompetence. When we are fired by passion and our inventions wow the world, we champion the innovating crusader. In some cases it does seem that this simplification is warranted. In many cases, however, this over-simplification fails to shed light on greater complexities that should be considered, even if not thoroughly understood. We *should* herald good individual leadership, but we should also recognize that leaders interact with one another and that results can rarely be ascribed to one leader alone. As Wilfred H. Drath at the Center for Creative Leadership has suggested: "More often, leadership has been expected to flow from a change in the individual competencies of individual leaders. The persistence of the obstacles to more inclusive and collective leadership comes from the failure to let go of long-held and long-valued assumptions about the individual nature of leadership."[7]

In some ways studying the differences between individual leadership and organizational leadership is like studying Newtonian mechanics and quantum dynamics. It doesn't require an understanding of quantum mechanics to place a person on the moon with a rocket, but understanding quantum complexities may significantly enhance our ability to create new opportunities of exploration. Newtonian forces tend to be more related to our everyday experience (think apples falling from trees, soccer balls bounding toward a goalie, guiding your vehicle through traffic). Quantum forces are most often described as "weird" (think of infinitely tiny bubbles called "quantum foam" as being the bedrock of the universe, or a single photon of light passing through two different slits simultaneously, or the idea that events are described as probabilities and become real and defined only when observed), and although such forces are understood to some degree by experts, their daily effects are imponderable. The observable, everyday experience of how a leader interacts with a group, how group dynamics work, and how people experience decisions and actions, explain causes and effects, and participate in learning is perhaps more like Newton's mechanics than quantum dynamics. Yet the range of variables for an organization that grows beyond roughly 150 people becomes too difficult to predict, even though many theorists have shed light upon the dynamic complexity. Grow a globally oriented organization with more than 200 or 300 people, and you begin to approach a need for a quantum viewpoint.

When Pfizer was completing tests for a blood pressure medication to help relieve angina, a female lab technician discovered that all the mice that had been given a certain formula had robust erections. No Pfizer scientist had been interested in this side effect, because it was not part of the intended research outcome, so they generally overlooked the lab tech's observations—that is, until clinical trials at V.A. hospitals began. Veterans were given the pills as part of the field trials concerning angina. The little blue pills were unexpectedly helping some of the men in the study who had trouble with impotence. They were having the same reactions noticed by the lab technician. As a result, the men began hoarding the pills.

"We found we couldn't get the pills back from the vets. Then doctors started finding pills missing from the hospital cabinets. Very quickly we learned the reason," said Pfizer vice president James Gardner during a Penn State presentation on the odd turns research can take. This unintended, and therefore disqualifying, effect became the central point of the product's success. The chemical that was failing clinical trials as an effective blood pressure regulator became Viagra. Weird. Unpredictable. And more common than we like to admit.[8] Cause-and-effect reasoning is good scientific method. But too much of it is Newtonian in nature, and it blinds us to the sometimes delightful outcomes of more quantumlike dynamics.

Physicists fervently suspect that Newton's mechanics and quantum dynamics are related, but the grand unification theory (some call it the "theory of everything") has eluded the brightest minds of the past century. However, we see the connections and believe one should inform the other. While Newton's equations may get us around the solar system fairly well, it will likely take Einstein's equations to help us move around the galaxy. In some ways this seems to be like individual versus organizational leadership. One should inform the other, but the connections are difficult to make, and therefore we tend to simplify leadership by limiting our view to individuals. As Katherine J. Klein and Steve W. J. Kozlowski suggest: "Although quick to acknowledge organizations as multilevel systems, organizational science has traditionally developed and tested theoretical models from three distinct points of view—organizational, group, and individual. Each level has become the province of different disciplines, theories, and approaches that have evolved over time. The current challenge is to integrate processes occurring

Diagram 1

across and within all levels of an organization that affect the behavior of individuals, groups, and organizations as a whole."[9]

Our meta-model, constructed from current mental models as well as historical research, integrates the forces between individual and organizational leadership and attempts to make sense of some of those connections.

Integration Model

LEADERS constantly confront the labors of authenticity, navigation, community, and architecture. As depicted in the graphical model on the previous page (Diagram 1), these four labors have been studied, classified, and researched, since the beginning of written history. These ideas are so common that they almost seem inadequate to explain everything. But we see them described in a straightforward manner all the time. In a 2004 Gartner Research article, Simon Mingay and his colleagues wrote: "Leadership is a capability that stands distinct from management. The latter focuses on execution, organization, planning, control, performance and ensuring continual improvement. Leadership involves direction; its specific concerns are vision, strategy, inspiration, motivation, values and culture."[10] While these authors define a classic separation of leadership and management, the article presumes an authentic leader and shows how vital leadership is to a successful IT operation. The statements connect readily with ideas of navigation and community. Although the authors suggest that continual improvement and execution are more managerial skills, we see them as essential leadership abilities.

It would be very exciting if we could show that these four classic labors corresponded directly to every leadership theory or research model, but no meta-model is that precise. These four classic labors do, however, account for the majority of research models and therefore grant us an opportunity to examine the ideas of individual and organizational leadership together rather than separately. It would be cool if authenticity were like gravity, navigation like electromagnetism, architecture like the weak nuclear force, and community like the strong nuclear force, but we would be in danger of forgetting our own advice about taking a metaphor one step too far.[11]

The subject of individual leadership dynamics can be considered Newtonian in the sense that it is well known, much studied, and corresponds with everyday common sense. Individual leadership refers to the qualities and abilities a person must demonstrate in order to earn modern respect as a leader and stimulate a followership. Management and leadership explanations are often very similar, and many overlap in terms of definition and behavioral expression, such as those described by Bernard Bass, Julian Birkenshaw, Ken Blanchard, Jim Collins, Steven Covey, Arthur Fiedler, John Gardner, Gary Hamel, Ronald Heifetz, Jim Kouzes and Barry Posner, Elizabeth Moss Kanter, John Kotter, John Maxwell, Simon Mingay, Henry Mintzberg, Tom Peters, Michael Porter, Noel Tichy, Manfred Kets de Vries, and nearly all other contemporary leadership researchers and pundits. These authors clearly describe the qualities and abilities that are deemed by constituents to be individually oriented.

Organizations are often thought of as complex living things, or ecological systems, and we support these vibrant metaphors, as they help describe a healthy range of contemplation regarding how organizations are born, grow, and sustain themselves over time. Organizational leadership can be likened to quantum dynamics in that the parts are well understood, the interactions sometimes defy commonsense understanding, and the connections to individual leadership are not always obvious. Organizational leadership refers to that set of practices that focus on the organization as a system and its relationship to the environment. It often triggers the internal conflicts that people feel when grappling with individual leadership interactions and organizational leadership interests. And organizational leadership relies upon a collective dynamic, an interaction of many, especially senior, leaders. The collective interaction weaves a fabric of organizational leadership that often results in a tapestry that is larger than any one person and that continues over a succession of individual leaders.

Four key labors of leaders, with their accompanying responsibilities and rewards, appear to be timeless, as each generation over recorded history has had to grapple more vigorously with one or more of these labors (See Table 2). Our meta-model integrates individual with organizational leadership using these four labors. The

Meta-model	Individual Focused on people	Organizational Focused on systems
Authenticity	Individual Marque	Organizational Marque
Navigation	Alignment	Adaptation
Architecture	High-Performance Work Systems	Dynamic Design
Community	Engagement	Perpetual Leadership

Table 2

ideas are straightforward but far from superficial. The boundaries between the two are not sharp, but are clear enough to make both demarcations as well as connections.

The remainder of this book will explore these ideas more fully, but in order to integrate individual and organizational leadership using the classic four labors model, one more level of description and perspective is required.

Timeless and Timely

WE SUGGEST that part of the synthesis, as well as the confusion, of leadership research, especially over the past century, has been caused not just by the application of various kinds of investigation, from psychological theory to anthropological observation, but also by the level of analysis. Often an entire theory of leadership that is assumed to encompass all levels of leadership responsibility is derived from examining only individual leadership actions over a very short time period. Or a well-known psychosocial construct is developed, and attempts are made to overextend its predictive properties to include too much of the range and nature of leadership responsibilities.

Fortunately, it is the very abundance of such investigation that shows the emergent pattern of our meta-model. By adding a type of time dimension to the model, the advantage of perspective is gained and yields a way of considering leadership that distills the ageless debates from the contemporary podcasts. The diagram on the following page (Table 3) shows what this looks like today. The four labors are timeless—Urukagina dealt with them long ago just as organizational leaders in all capacities deal with them today. Contemporary issues like emotional maturity, distinction, and widespread commitment are timely expressions of some aspect of the four labors. These smaller-scale issues become heated topics that often consume a disproportionate amount of attention.

Using this perspective allows us to place many contemporary issues into the appropriate leadership context. During the transactional age of leadership development, the pressing community issue was finding and training people as work evolved from an agricultural mode to a factory one. In the transformational age, strategic planning was the central navigational issue, and adaptation considerations were simply described as contingency planning. And the emphasis for high-performance work systems in our transcultural age is symptomatic of a concern for creating an innovation environment, whereas during the transformational age the leadership concern was creating an environment where quality could be improved.

With this perspective, we can now amplify a bit on our timeless foundational leadership ideas and explain more succinctly how individual and organizational leadership responsibilities integrate within each of the four labors.

Authenticity

PEOPLE often ask themselves, "What impact will I have upon the world? Will my life leave a mark? Will I make a difference?" The answers to these questions are partly determined by people's responses to leadership opportunities. Choosing to lead offers the chance to have a personal impact. This is the essential idea we are trying to convey with the use of the word *marque*. Marque is variously described as a brand, a symbol of a brand, or the symbols or actions associated with a brand. It is even at times referred to as the boundary between things. We believe that individual leaders, as well as organizations, have brand identities. The question both followers

Meta-model		Dimension	Contemporary Critical Outcomes
Authenticity	Individual	Individual Marque	Presence Reliability Emotional Maturity
	Organizational	Organizational Marque	Pervasive Values Trusted Brand Distinction Corporate
Navigation	Individual	Alignment	Crystal-Clear Direction Widespread Commitment Purposeful Action
	Organizational	Adaptation	Scanning Systems Opportunistic Bias Premeditated Agility
Architecture	Individual	High-Performance Work Systems	Creative Tension Rampant Virtuosity Continuous Play
	Organizational	Dynamic Design	Matchless Business Model Seamless Structure Flawless Mission – Critical Systems
Community	Individual	Engagement	Genuinely Appreciated Specifically Enabled Appropriately Accountable
	Organizational	Perpetual Leadership	Fertile Environment Robust Development Excess Talent

Timeless, stable, leadership foundational ideas.

Timelier, fluid, expressions of current leadership needs.

Table 3

of individual leaders and users of organizational products or services ask is, "Is this brand the real thing?" In terms of living inside organizations, individual leaders often ask themselves, "Where are the boundaries between me and the organization? Where's the overlap? Do I fit in?"

In his book *Authentic Leadership*, Medtronic CEO Bill George recounts his development and growth as an individual leader, and describes his company's growth as a brand and even its battles with the FDA. At the beginning of the book, he declares his beliefs, which have been hard earned over a lifetime of struggle, work, and contemplation: "I believe that leadership begins and ends with authenticity. It's being yourself; being the person you were created to be... Authentic leaders use their natural abilities, but they also recognize their shortcomings and work hard to overcome them. They lead with purpose, meaning, and values... Authentic leaders are dedicated to developing themselves because they know that becoming a leader takes a lifetime of personal growth."[12]

Throughout the rest of his book, George reconfirms and expands upon this theme of uncompromising authenticity. The marque of a leader is about a commitment to values, of role modeling, of clarifying personal values through defining moments of leadership action. Recall that in our brief description of the transactional leadership period, traits and abilities were the first identifying factors researchers investigated. We have a deep need to know whether or not leaders possess commonly held traits and characteristics. Many of these traits have been documented, and many debates have arisen over the exact number or kind of traits or characteristics that exist, and even whether or not they are universal. The unifying concept underlying this research and debate has to do with authenticity. Are you who you purport to be? And will that marque, that personal brand, stimulate others to follow?

Just as leaders create a brand image, like it or not, so do organizations. The collective experience of thousands of interactions is how organizational leaders determine the overall level of organizational authenticity, even though each individual act is how customers or employees determine their experience. Organizations are weighed by their authentic actions as readily as individuals are.

Having an organizational reputation is no more discretionary than having an individual reputation.

Peter Georgescu, the former CEO of Young & Rubicon, echoes Bill George's argument. He recounts his experience of individual leadership growth but expands the thesis of authenticity to include the authentic company. His idea is that organizational leaders must look at organizational authenticity, questions of ethics, and brand as more than mere image manipulation. "Success now has as much to do with who you are, the unique and moral character your people bring to their work, and the way it governs the way you care for customers—because that trustworthy character is what customers look for now in a company."[13]

Tom Peters labels this tension as "Brand Inside: Brand Outside."[14] His thoughts on the subject raise the following questions: Are we authentic to the core, or is brand identity simply glorified marketing? Is the brand experience that customers have the same quality and kind as employees have? Does each associate possess the entire brand DNA, and is it reflected in their work? All of these questions are about one thing: authenticity.

Navigation

IT IS commonly argued that an individual leader's responsibility is to inspire his or her followers to believe in and support a distinctive, unifying set of goals that lead to a desirable destination. Some people suggest that navigation begins with a good central idea that explains why the business exists and how it will add value.[15] Others suggest that leaders have dual roles—vision and architecture. The vision part concerns direction setting, providing meaning, and triggering imagination, while the architecture part involves how to structure an organization that can get to the destination.[16] Some people argue that visionaries and visionary companies don't remain visionary forever and that they seldom live beyond their first strategy. Those in this camp argue more strenuously for strategy as the operative idea behind navigation.[17] Others suggest that leaders must both envision exciting futures and enlist other people to share in the passion to work toward reaching those futures.[18] We would agree that leaders navigate the waters of meaning as well as the waters of strategy. And the primary task for the individual leader-as-navigator is to create an alignment of vision and strategy—a belief in the central idea that moves the organization forward.

Navigation involves conceptualizing where we are going and how we will get there, but it also requires articulation, often in inspiring and meaningful ways. To gain alignment, goals must be important enough to lift people out of their petty preoccupations and inspire them to want to contribute their best efforts. How many petty preoccupations consume your followers? Do you have silo constipation in your organization? How about engagement problems? How about a loss of meaning to the work that people do day in, day out? How about extrinsic rewards manipulation being the major force that drives them to the goal? Are these factors sufficient to call upon their best efforts?

The organizational leader must also adapt to new realities. Destinations may remain relatively more constant than strategies, but even destinations for organizations change. In this transcultural age, global leadership pressures are making organizations recalibrate their ultimate goals or visions of who they are or where they are ultimately going. In *The Future and Its Enemies*, Virginia Postrel puts the question of adaptation this way: "Do we search for stasis—a regulated, engineered world? Or do we embrace dynamism—a world of constant creation, discovery and competition?...These two poles, stasis and dynamism, increasingly define our political, intellectual and cultural landscape."[19] Is your organization trying to maintain control against a changing landscape or learning to adapt to a fluid ecology? How much adaptation must take place? Is your organization's internal rate of change sufficient to take advantage of the environmental rate of change? Do you need to wholly reconceptualize what your organization is about?

These questions have been explored by many authors, such as C. K. Prahald and Venkat Ramaswamy in their book, *The Future of Competition*. They pose the adaptation question this way: "Thus, the paradox of the twenty-first-century economy: Consumers have more choices that yield less satisfaction. Top management has more strategic options that yield less value. Are we on the cusp of a new industrial system with characteristics different from those we now

take for granted?"[20] The slippery sameness of products and processes provided by a transcultural age invites a high cycle rate of
align-adapt-realign-readapt. For many leaders, navigating has never
been as difficult as it is today. The incessant forces of change make
the effort to navigate seem futile, so leaders often default to a "throw
a bunch of stuff at the wall and see what sticks" strategy, or they
develop bold goals and when the strategy course succeeds, they continue along it, making as much as possible of the commercial waters
they are in before wind, current, tide, and storm force them to
change course. If they successfully ride out the change, they seek
new places to plunder. If they are unsuccessful, they break apart or
capsize. Or if simply damaged and weak, they are boarded by others
who increase their fleet through acquisition.

Architecture

THE FUNDAMENTAL idea of leader-as-architect is easy to see. Leaders
build business models that allow their goals to be realized, institute
systems and processes to support these models, and create structure
and roles for individuals so that work flows are optimized. Leader-
as-architect creates some confusion for leadership students because
the basic ideas seem more management oriented in nature. But they
are not. Cost, quality, time to market, continual improvement, mis-
sion-critical systems—these and many more ideas come to mind as
what individual leaders work on with their followers. Many of these
concerns become functional in nature, which is why they seem to
have more to do with management than with leadership. The natural
evolution of functional specialty often limits individual leaders from
expanding their organizational leadership abilities. They become
highly effective individual leaders in a functional area but fail to
grow wider organizational leadership abilities. Or because of their
functional specialization, they become effective at organizational
leadership but never develop effective individual leadership skills.

For example, "continuous improvement," "engaging in new challenges," "thinking outside the box," or other phrases that deal with
new and higher-performing systems, processes, or products are
documented throughout leadership research. Researchers focus
specifically upon one or another favorite topic, such as creativity,

innovation, process improvement, and execution. The thrust of the leadership effort required for any one of these is *how to create an environment where constant improvement can occur*. This is the architectural work of the individual leader. The confusion as to whether or not this is management and leadership work is based on the work itself. The management question involves creating the high-performance work systems. The leadership question relates to developing the environment in which high-performance work systems can be perfected. The thesis of Michael Schrage's provocative book *Serious Play* addresses this dichotomy directly. Most thinking about high-performance work systems, he argues, has to do with the invention or application of some new technology, often of an IT nature. But Schrage's work at MIT's media lab showed him that changing behavior was more important than changing technology. And behavior change is best encouraged by focusing on the environment, not on work.[21]

Organizational leadership focuses on the whole architectural system and requires an eye for and expertise in dynamic design. Organizational design has become a specialized discipline over the past twenty years. Many people write about how organizational leaders need to work at continually refreshing the organization by changing its design, an idea often referred to as *strategic reorganization*. This is the natural architectural consequence of what happens when leaders adapt to new realities. Amy Kates, a management consultant who specializes in this type of strategic realignment, suggests, "A fundamental principle of organization design is that a change in strategy requires a new set of capabilities and a realignment of the core elements of the organization."[22]

Individual leadership in the architectural arena involves creating an environment where constant improvement can be achieved, even during strategic realignment. Regardless of the realignment, the principles for creating a culture of innovation, of high-performance work systems, does not vary much. Organizational leadership dynamically considers the basic architecture or structure of the organization and aligns it as navigational adaptation changes occur. Disagreeing with early organizational design theorists who believed design was solely the province of senior management, David Nadler and Michael Tushman argue, "Organization design needs to be done both ways—designing top down to implement the strategy and then, within the context of that design, designing from the bottom up to improve basic work processes and create meaningful and motivating jobs for individuals."[23]

Modern organizations that grapple with architectural concerns in this manner—a combined top-down and bottom-up approach—are exercising appropriate individual and organizational leader-as-architect muscles. Doing so calls for greater coordination and feedback systems in order for architecture to work, which is often why it seems to take longer and sometimes feels inefficient, but organizations that have developed the muscle tend to have more vibrant organizations.

Community

SINCE leadership is a relationship-oriented phenomenon, most of the research and writing on the subject has concerned the leader/follower interaction. There are a number of leadership perspectives that revolve solely around this leader-as-community-builder dimension. Also springing from the labor of community is the idea of *followership*, which examines the impact of followers upon leaders. As Ira Chaleff expresses it: "All important social accomplishments require complex group effort, and therefore, leadership and followership. Both are necessary in the pursuit of a common purpose. Some believe that influence in the leader-follower relationship is largely one-way. This is far from true. Followers have great capacity to influence leaders."[24]

During the transactional period of business history, extrinsic exchanges between leader and follower were studied: *If I give more of certain kinds of extrinsic benefits to my followers, or if I provide more goal direction, will they produce more in return?* During the transformational period the question became: *How can I better empower followers and help them feel more able to contribute via providing greater information, authority, and discretion?* The current transcultural period, however, poses the question in a manner that subsumes the other two periods: *How do I create an environment of possibilities that engage followers to want to extend their best efforts?*

In fact, some would argue that in the transcultural period this labor of leadership follows a line of reasoning that is wonderfully illustrated by Tom Peters:

> Leaders-Teachers Do *Not* "Transform People"! Instead leaders-mentors-teachers (1) *provide a context* which is marked by (2) *access to a luxuriant portfolio of meaningful opportunities* (projects) which (3) *allow people to fully* (and safely, mostly—caveat: "they" don't engage unless they're "mad about something") *express their innate curiosity* and (4) *engage in a vigorous discovery voyage* (alone and in small teams, assisted by an extensive self-constructed network) by which those people (5) *go to—create places they* (and their mentors-teachers-leaders) *had never dreamed existed*—and then the leaders-mentors-teachers (6) *applaud like hell, stage "photo-ops," and ring the church bells 100 times to commemorate the bravery of their "followers'" explorations!*[25]

Peters expresses many of the fundamental ideas of the leadership labor of community through his unique voice. Individual leadership grapples with the engagement issue—not rewards alone, not accountability alone, not empowerment alone, but overall engagement. The Gallup Management Group has been instrumental in recent times in creating focus on engagement. They do this through sifting their interview database and considering three different engagement terms: *engaged, disengaged, and actively disengaged.*[26] Fundamentally, engaged individuals are passionately connected to the organization and help drive it forward. Disengaged individuals sleepwalk through their work or simply do a fair day's work for a fair day's pay. Actively disengaged workers deploy their time and energy to undermine the organization. Although these descriptions are provocative, they do not adequately address the question of what individual leadership is required to do in order to produce engagement.

Organizational leadership lifts its gaze from engagement to perpetual leadership. The community question for organizational leaders is how to build a process or system that will continue to offer the organization with next-generation leadership candidates. As the late Peter Drucker first noted during the mid-1990s, business continuity is being threatened by a lack of competent successors because of a paucity of good leadership development.[27] In response to this threat, major universities have either shifted or reinforced their focus on leadership development activities to look at the entire process of developing next-generation leaders. Harvard Business School's Rakesh Khurana suggests, "What really matters are systems that develop and perpetuate talent. We're focusing on the systems that build people."[28]

Organizational Equilibrium

ORGANIZATIONS are far from static. They often seem more quantum than Newtonian in their dynamism and unpredictability. This is one of the most distinguishing differences between individual leadership and organizational leadership. Individual leadership is most often experienced and acquired during a period of time associated with one of three things: a short-term project, a crisis situation, or a period in elected office. Yet all of these individually led cases exist in a larger context or as part of a larger organizational setting. Simplifying them to study the individual interactions is warranted, but we must go beyond this to understand organizational dynamics.

In our graphic model (see pg. 12), the banded lines between the three labors are meant to represent dynamism. Change strategy, and it creates changes in community and architecture. Reorganize, and corresponding effects will be felt in community and navigation. Change hiring practices or team dynamics, and new architecture will likely be required, and in some cases even changes in strategy will occur. Experience an authenticity breach, and the entire system is jolted. Organizational leadership requires a systems view. It requires a level of comprehension that goes beyond a personal relationship to a known set of individuals, to the relationships of all individuals to one another and to the organizational purpose. Because of the inherent complexities of these interactions and their sometimes quantumlike weirdness, organizational leaders need to strive to create organizational equilibrium—that is, balance and momentum between the four labors that allows the organization to operate well. Organizational leaders should also understand that equilibrium is a difficult state to achieve—many factors can alter an optimum equilibrium. This requires greater amounts of tolerance for ambiguity, patience for alterations to take effect, and openness for the unexpected weirdness that can make the difference. Those who apply

Newtonian measures to complex organizations blind themselves and their constituents to complexity's gifts. Instead of understanding why the little blue pills are being stolen, we simply instigate greater security measures.

The subsequent chapters will take each component of our model in turn and make the links between individual and organizational leadership. These labors of leaders are timeless, and our current world economy has provided an abundance of responses to them. Ignoring, attempting to bypass, or simply not fully understanding these labors is dangerous and suggests that either inattention or inexperience is at work.

Mental Models

TRYING to create a type of unification model between individual and organizational leadership is ambitious, and our model is imperfect, as all models are. But as neurologist and author V. S. Ramachandran points out: "Our brains are essentially model-making machines. We need to construct useful, virtual reality simulations of the world that we can act on."[29] We construct mental models automatically for everything from how to organize housework to global brand strategies. But all mental models are approximations of reality. Some are more reliable, more consistent with obtaining predictable results, more helpful than others. We need mental models, and yet even the most durable mental models are flawed in some way.

We believe this is why we often simplify our mental models as best we can in order to test them and over time rely upon the patterns that seem to be the most predictable. More complex models, or systems models, are difficult, but perhaps not too difficult to consider. In his 2002 acceptance speech for the prestigious Jay Forrester Award for the best contributions to systems thinking over the preceding five years, John Sterman, an MIT Sloan Management School professor, asked: "Is system dynamics science, engineering, or applied mathematics? Is it social science? Is it a philosophy? Is it a form of consulting, a theory of action? Is it hard or soft? The difficulty in answering the question 'what is system dynamics' arises not because we don't know which of these things it is, but because it is all these things and more."[30]

Like Sterman, we accept that our model is part science and part philosophy, supported by research and conclusions drawn from years of consulting fieldwork, and that it contains both new and familiar ideas. We hope it is interesting enough to tickle your mind and open your mental models for examination, stimulation, and perhaps renewal. Our belief is that developing leaders well requires a meditation on the nature of leadership as much as applying contemporary techniques to temporary conditions.

2 *Authenticity*

CREDIBILITY, integrity, honesty, competence, and genuineness are the domain of authenticity—the first noticed, most studied, and least forgiven labor of leadership. This labor is perhaps most subject to individual experience and personal assessment. Each and every follower reserves the right to judge whether or not an individual leader is the real thing. Each and every consumer, supplier, partner, or nation reserves the right to judge, day by day, whether or not the actions, intentions, or deeds of another organization, whether small company or government, are authentic. We judge authenticity every day, action by action, intention by intention. Constituents and consumers hold leaders and organizations under constant surveillance with an eye toward a slip of credentials, a false intention, or poor conduct. And when the authenticity alarm trips, solid waste hits the rotary blades.

The Western world's competency-crazed viewpoint tends to judge behavior as not just the most important consideration, but often the *only* consideration. We prudently and fairly ask one another if a person's or organization's actions are sufficiently authentic— meaning whether the person or organization has acted according to public statements of what they claim they will or will not do. We often refer to this as "walking your talk." This idea is common in a variety of languages. The Germans say, *"Taten sagen mehr als Worte,"* which translated means "acts say more than words." In Afghanistan it is said, "If you think you are leading and no one is following you, then you are only taking a walk." And in China the idea can be represented in at least two different ways: *"yan xing yi zhi,"* meaning "words actions one together," or *"xing dong sheng yu yu yan,"* meaning "actions win, or are stronger than, language."[1]

In order to do what you say you will do, you must have something to say. Actions may speak louder than words, but all actions originate in words, spoken or silent, deliberate or unintentional, hastily conceived or baked over a lifetime. A leader's interior life

29

may not be well constructed, maturely developed, or filled with good intentions toward others, but it exists, and this interior life is the source of a leader's words and intentions. Congruence between exterior behavior and interior conditions, between thoughts and deeds, is central to leadership in all cultures. We don't just judge whether or not leaders do what they say they will do, but we also judge whether or not their intentions in doing so are good or bad. We evaluate whether or not customer service is provided as a compulsory action of rote learned behavior, or as a reflection of behavior matched with deeper intention. Actions, deeds, and behaviors are simply the exterior dimension of authenticity evaluation. We also judge intentions, motivations, and other less tangible, more interior items that are more difficult to fathom, let alone measure. We judge words, even those that are unspoken.

But even if organizational development specialists or marketing analysts cannot easily create measurements for the intentions of a person or organization, this does not mean that human beings fail to assess them. Interior factors are significant when establishing and maintaining an authentic framework from which followers or customers (who are simply a larger constituency of followers in a sense) make holistic judgments concerning authenticity.

These ideas are so powerful, so timeless, that they help change the meaning of words over time. For example, take the word *brand*. For centuries during the agrarian age, people throughout the world branded cattle, sheep, and horses as a means of identifying ownership. During the industrial age, the idea of identification was altered a bit when clothing manufacturers began placing marks of identification, or authentication, upon cloth or clothing goods. Artists and producers of cabinetry, pottery (from bisque to porcelain), glassware, and even weaponry started placing marks of origin, artist, or reputation, in addition to marks of ownership, upon their goods. It became important to identify not just exteriors—where was it manufactured, who made it, how well it was made, what process was used in its making—but also interiors—what was the reputation, intention, motivation, aesthetic quality, and attitude of the maker toward the craft and eventual consumer of the work. In the collectibles world, identifying authentic from replicated artifacts is an art and science in itself, and one important source of authentication is the brand mark.

An example of this can be found with Ming dynasty porcelain, considered by many to be the finest period of porcelain manufacture. During the Ming period, porcelain quality varied to a degree, and experts often consider Suen-tih (1426–1436) to be the best, followed by Ching-hwa (1465–1488), Yung-lo (1403–1425), and Keatsing (1522–1567). The emperor approved a *nian hao*, or period mark, that was used to identify Imperial porcelain. This mark seems to have been made and used during the Ming dynasty period only by a small number of highly specialized artists, who may have spent a significant portion of their time making the marks. There were not many of these special "brand markers," and the handwriting of a few individual painters can be recognized, which aids in the identification of authentic Imperial Ming porcelain. This is part of a more intricate and often laborious effort to distinguish copied marks of nonofficial Imperial Ming porcelain, which greatly outnumber the officially marked ones. It appears Ching-hwa was the most copied.[2]

During the modern age, call it the information age, the word *brand* has altered a bit once again. No longer just a mark of owner-ship or origin, it now means something like "to impress unforget-tably upon one's mind." Individual and organizational brand identity become paramount in this issue of authenticity—the question of whether or not we are getting the real thing. In a world where serv-ice rivals—even, arguably, exceeds—quality as the most important aspect of a brand, this emphasis on impressing unforgettably contin-ues to develop our appreciation of interiors as well as exteriors. While in the Ming period there were many fine-quality reproduc-tions created—porcelain of arguably similar quality but lacking an authentic Imperial mark to distinguish it—in today's world we judge the manufacture of goods and services not just by the quality of goods or services received, but also by the intentions of their providers.

Business periodicals frequently cite cases of quality products being lax in interior components. Issues of child labor, environmen-tal insensitivity, workers' rights, and cultural nuance are reason enough for some consumers to permanently lose faith in a brand. Copying brand products and the protection of intellectual property in its various forms has become a common business issue. The lasting impression of authentic or copy, good intention or poor intention, good behavior or bad behavior, interiors aligned with exteriors all combine in an algorithm that informs the constituents' or consumers' unforgettable impression. Failure or success often follows that impression.

A North American case in point involves ExxonMobil Corporation. The 1989 Valdez oil spill soured many consumers on Exxon products. To this day there are those who will not refuel at Exxon pumps. Perhaps some of these people were among those protesters who cut their credit cards into the shape of a fish and mailed them to Exxon headquarters after the spill. For a time, Exxon received thousands of returned, destroyed credit cards every day.

The essential argument surrounding the spill centered on who was at fault and who should fix the problem. Although Exxon had a clearly documented procedure for handling such incidents, and although the issue at hand was in part a legal one as to who was responsible for the oil while in transit, consumers tried Exxon in the court of public opinion and the company's authenticity was found guilty. Well-informed businesspeople may empathize with the pinch Exxon was in at the time, but the issue at stake was simple: Exxon's inaction during the critical stages of the spill was interpreted by consumers as a lack of intention to keep the environment safe. Generations of MBA students have reviewed this case study along with similar famous ones concerning products made by Johnson & Johnson, Parmalat, Intel, Perrier, as well as various automobile manufacturers, clothing brands, and cosmetics makers. Exxon as an organization has moved past its perhaps most infamous chronicle and has incorporated many methods of enhancing its interior conditions of environmental concern.[3] But even today, for many consumers the unforgettable impression is indelibly settled.

Individual Authenticity

THE GOALS of many competency-based leadership development efforts are noble and well intentioned. Organizations conduct internal audits of best practices using a variety of methods. Or they contract with external experts to cast a net across an industry of best practices to find and apply those that best match their situation. Or they purchase high-quality, behaviorally oriented, research-based developmental material from leadership development researchers and suppliers. In all of these cases the intention is to find measurements that allow people inside an organization to assess their abilities and engage in developmental activities that will enhance their ability to increase their leadership effectiveness. At best, competency-based behavioral modification of this sort has been shown to be wonderfully effective when instituted by well-intentioned, thoroughly knowledgeable professionals in the organizational and leadership development field; it helps people improve their leadership abilities—in some cases in significant ways. However, when not handled well, or used as the only path to leadership development, it can backfire and tend to create a culture of competency cloning that not only does not improve behavior, but also leads constituents to deride the attempt at wholesale behavioral modification. Constituents in this case may rebel against or reject the forced training, even though they may engage in behavioral sycophancy for the rewards offered. Such leadership mimicry can be deadly.

Behavioral change is imperative, but it deals only with exteriors. We would argue that the best-intentioned and perhaps best-received developmental experiences are not those that result in people seeing how they can become cookie-cutter exemplars of a static set of behaviors, but rather those that inspire them to become the best version, the most authentic version, of who they really are as they add or enhance well-researched behaviors to their repertoire. Such experiences invite the leader to make an archeological exploration of both interiors and exteriors in order to more fully awake themselves to their potential, their desires, their true intentionality, and their ability to overcome the exciting, sometimes brutal demands of modern leadership.

This approach to leadership development is usually more powerful, lasts longer, and yields greater results. It often requires more time and effort as well, which is why it is often diluted, truncated, or not used at all. The totalitarian grip of behavioral theory is now relaxing to include a wider range of additional theoretical perspective, but its long-term influence upon corporations is immense. The belief that behavior is the only thing that matters plays into the bias that corporations have toward expediency and objectivity. If we can create best practices for how to ship products, then why can't we do the same for shipping leaders? If we can describe leadership behaviorally, then let's write the training manual, spell out exactly what the behaviors should be, and leave any interior development up to the individual. Do motives or intentions matter if the exterior behavioral pattern is met?

Most mature businesspeople see the lack of sensibility in this argument, even when they make decisions about leadership development that reinforce behavior-only processes. The investigation of our interiors—our values, motives, intentions, desires, passions, hopes, dreams—all of this is not just fair territory for leaders, but it is also critical to leadership development. As Manfred Kets de Vries, program director at INSEAD, observes: "The catalyst of much of our behavior lies beneath consciousness. Most people don't like to hear this observation, because they see bowing to unconscious motivation as a sign of weakness. That reaction is understandable ... But like it or not, we all have 'blind spots,' and our challenge is to find out what they're all about."[4]

Character development is an important issue in leadership development these days, despite its often colliding with the production of results. Such development is vital. Each level of leadership consciousness and ability builds a foundation from which the next level of ability can be developed. And after gaining competence at that level, the person can integrate with, not just move to, the next level of leadership consciousness, ability, and influence. Each successive level of ability from individual to organizational leadership embraces and encompasses those that come before it. These abilities don't disappear any more than high-school algebra disappears for an engineer when he or she begins using differential equations to solve important technical problems. The abilities are integrated into a larger context, not lost and discarded like snakeskin.

Opinions abound on the process of developing a sense of self, a deep understanding of our authentic nature. Psychologists, organizational development specialists, philosophers, journalists, theologians, CEOs, and anthropologists of every ilk have penned their views on authenticity. But as John H. Humphreys and Walter O. Einstein have pointed out, "Although motivation, leadership, and personality each offer an extensive literature, [we] must attempt to grasp the intricacies of each."[5]

In a nutshell, there are four prevailing concepts that should be considered for leadership development. First, development is not a monologue, but a dialogue. In other words, humans not only grow and acquire self-meaning and self-identity through inward study and the happenstances of biology. They also develop their self-concept through interaction with others, especially those people who are important in their lives. Second, our self-concept, our construct of authenticity, is shaped by the personal choices we make during critical, or defining, moments in our lives. This means we exercise choice over the work we engage in; we create meaning from the manner in which we handle opportunities; and we evaluate the effort we put into our own experience, all of which counts significantly toward our authenticity. This series of engagements simultaneously shape and reveal what is commonly known as personal values. Third, deep motivational issues, regardless of sculpting processes or pressures, significantly influence our leadership decisions. And finally, our natural talents enable and restrict the range of leadership roles we will most likely play over a long period of time.

The following diagram (Diagram 2) is our way of visualizing this situation. The wide top part of the inverted cone represents behaviors, in all their nuances. A wide range of behaviors can be exhibited that derive from a smaller number of natural talents, driven by even smaller numbers of values and motivations. The cone represents this decreasing progression of items and indicates that natural talents may be assessed or viewed more easily than values, which are more evident and visible—both to ourselves and others—than our deeper motivations, which may lie in unconscious arenas, as we have explained.

Leadership development is enhanced when the process allows people to take a variety of deep dives into each of these layers of self. Like an archeological dig, examining each layer is fascinating in and of itself, but each layer also helps to make more sense of those above and below it. Long-term behavioral change is best produced when

LEVELS OF AWARENESS

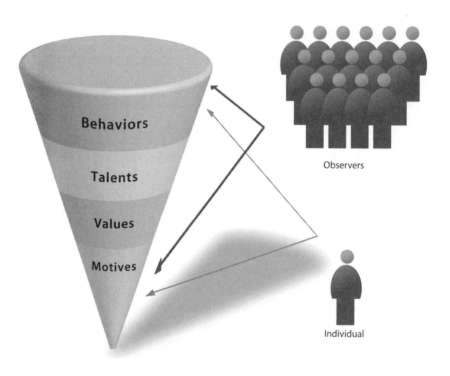

Diagram 2

people understand their underlying talents, values, and motives. This contextualization is not merely a nice thing to do, but in our opinion it is also imperative.

Digging for the Self

CLARITY of self is one of many objectives for conducting an archeological dig below the behavioral surface of a leader's persona. From this clarity a person has the basis to formulate a strategy for improvement. The ability to reflect, to develop identity/consciousness/self-concept, and to evaluate this construct over time, as well as at particular times, is unique to humans. Indeed, we all come to grips with who we really are at different points in our lives. The more mature we are, the more honest with ourselves we tend to be. As we evolve, we often have to mine the layers of our evolution to gain new perspective, new insight into this self-construct. In fact, maturing leaders know that as they gain more confidence, experience, breadth of knowledge, willingness to adapt, and eagerness to seek and accept challenges, what lies behind has prepared them for what lies ahead. Ken Wilber concludes, "[T]he self has the capacity to intimately identify with a level of consciousness, become competent at that level, and then disidentify with it (and integrate it) in order to step up to the next higher and wider sphere."[6]

In effect, leadership development can help people increase their ability to integrate their various archeological layers, as well as the content of their life's episodes. This accelerates the ability to gain a more stable sense of identity and reconcile conflicts or mild, everyday types of delusions we all have that help us cope with the realities of who we are in the world. The wisdom of self-reflection is ancient. Marcus Aurelius, known as the last of the so-called five good emperors of the Roman Empire, wrote often about the value of self-examination.[7] His writings are simply a part of a greater heritage of thought on self-contemplation. Abraham Lincoln never took a Myers-Briggs assessment; Elizabeth I never asked for a 360 Report; and Gandhi, to our knowledge, never went on a whitewater leadership retreat. Yet each of these leaders considered their true identity and purpose with rare honesty, questioning both their leadership role and the effect they had upon their times.

Modernity has provided a host of thought leadership on the subject of self-examination, ranging from recaps of earlier works, to postmodern views that authenticity is a social construct and therefore has fluid properties that make it susceptible to so much rubbish, to extreme permissive views that suggest being who you really are is all that counts, even if the real you is a pretty miserable, immature, and self-absorbed person. We tend to agree with the more mainstream view that leaders develop when they engage in a mature examination of true selfhood and how they interact with the world. As Kets de Vries has observed, "[A] good sense of identity allows a person to feel good in their skin—that is, in a state of effective balance between their emotional and physiological inner and outer worlds."[8]

A person's identity can only rise above the trivial or the self-absorbed if his or her aspirations are commensurate with things that matter beyond the personal. This idea is the genesis of many lucid and evocative arguments that leaders should expand their awareness of time, place, occasion, issue, and opportunity in order to place self in a larger context. This allows them greater opportunity to develop more robust aspirations and seek potential leadership opportunities. These opportunities could result from the demands of nature, of meeting other human needs, of responding to a religious calling, of acting on the duties of citizenship, of helping grow an economy, or of some other worthy cause that provides a service to self and others.

This greater context serves not only the individual leader, but the organizational leader as well. Just as the self and a band of constituents are moved by context, so too can the collective body or the organization. A leader aspires to move others to greatness, as both an individual and organizational leader. The leader who acts "in the stream of history" feels called and compelled to create personal and organizational meaning.[9] The person who aspires to lead as a manifestation of self-mastery will more likely resist the seductive call of power and the disaster of self-destruction. This leader will lay claim to the reality that during his history upon the planet, his deeds counted for something worthwhile. And if the stars align, and this leader's authentic impact is felt, perhaps he or she "will meet with a success unexpected in common hours."[10]

Much has been written about the development of the authentic self, and professional lives have been devoted to the examination of the various levels of, as well as the resistances to, authentic self-development. More ideas on these topics can be found in the notes section and appendix.

Contemporary Outcomes for Individual Authenticity

Making the case for establishing an individual marque as a leader is easy. It is the most directly observable manifestation of the labor of authenticity. Each generation tests its ideas, beliefs, and postures as to this labor, and we suggest that in recent times the following three critical outcomes have the most currency:

PRESENCE

RELIABILITY

EMOTIONAL MATURITY

Presence

THE ISSUE of presence has been pinging the radar screens of many human resources professionals as senior leaders cry for help—usually not for themselves, but for others whom they believe lack sufficient presence. The beauty of this outcome seems to be in the eye of the beholder, but we think we can describe some of the more basic elements of presence.

One business journalist concluded that executive presence "refers to that ability to take hold of a room by making a polished entrance, immediately shaking people's hands, and forging quick, personal connections instead of defaulting to robotic formalism and shrinking into a chair. When leaders with executive presence speak, people listen—because the talk is filled with conviction instead of equivocation. They inspire that I'll-follow-you-anywhere loyalty, conveying an aura of warmth and authenticity to everybody from the receptionist to the CEO."[11] A consultant examined good versus great CEO candidates and listed three major areas in which the great excel—management savvy, political intelligence, and personal style. He concluded that elite candidates help constituents feel appreciated, don't appear to be self-serving, make the right judgments about where to expend energy, and make success look effortless.[12]

We reviewed more than a dozen companies' offerings that specialize in helping executives develop presence. In some cases the work focused nearly exclusively on communication issues, such as techniques for relaxing under pressure, managing energy, using expression to add the "human touch" to messages, organizing messages, and delivering emotional impact. Some of these programs included assessments geared to helping people focus on their specific communication issues through practices designed to help them learn new behaviors. Others literally specialized in helping managers gain more upward influence, navigate corporate politics, gain access to promotions, and solicit greater support for projects and programs. Nearly all of these techniques appealed to those who had aspirations for gaining top leadership positions.

We agree with the ideas about authentic communication but niggle a bit over the ideas that lend themselves to corporate ladder climbing.

Reliability

As EARLY as 1915 the relationship between leadership and personal attributes such as responsibility, integrity, conviction, ambition, credibility, and self-confidence were being evaluated. Research findings during the transactional era indicated that the reliable leader was not just personally reliable—meaning conscientious, dependable, and committed—but was also able to consistently create conditions for followers that led to the cooperative completion of tasks and the achievement of desirable goals. These personal traits and abilities were studied again during the transformational era, and although the same basic findings were confirmed, the expanded list of personality or personal traits showed that reliable leaders also possessed relevant intelligence, vision-making abilities, better-than-average communication skills, higher-than-average levels of cognitive skills and creative abilities, and better-than-average levels of interpersonal skills. The transcultural era tends to extend this list to include applying all of these traits or abilities to multicultural situations and the ability to work effectively in a diverse, networked environment.

These personal qualities of reliability are often reduced to the single idea of "getting the job done." This aspect of reliability, however, often comes into conflict with other leadership abilities, as getting the job done can often be accomplished with poorer leadership qualities that are effective only in the short term. Reliability has both task and social qualities that often compete for dominance, and the most highly regarded leaders are those who are able to demonstrate reliability in both domains.

Jim Collins's work on level-five leaders suggests that reliability is best achieved when the ambitions of goal attainment are coupled with a mature faith in the collective abilities of the organization.[13] Other emotional intelligence or social intelligence researchers ratify this sentiment and suggest that emotional qualities more often than not define whether the leader is considered level five or four or less.

The pressure of short-term economic goal accomplishment is severe. Perhaps more than any other time in history, short-term economic analyses provided by market analysts from outside the organization stress the goal-accomplishment side of reliability's equation. A compensatory amount of social intelligence is required to deal with this economic siege.

Emotional Maturity

EMOTIONAL or social intelligence has gained a large portion of executive and human resources attention over the past decade. While maturity in general has always been seen as an expectation of increased leadership authority and is often broadly associated with aging, its status has gained more importance as the effects of maturity have been documented in comparison to organizational success. What is surprising about this renewed interest in developing greater maturity is not that it has been shown by research to be effective, but that organizations and senior leaders have generally lost sight of the fact that strategic intellect and execution alone are not the sole—nor even, perhaps, the primary—factors for success. Daniel Goleman, a popular author in this arena of investigation, bluntly observes, "The art of sustained leadership is getting others to produce superior work, and high IQ alone is insufficient to the task."[14]

Emotional maturity is a significant ally in helping others to want to produce superior work. But there are times when the whole emotional intelligence phenomenon is overstated and perhaps overrated. Defining, measuring, and developing greater emotional maturity can be enhanced through training, but deep maturity actually happens far more gradually and often requires leaders to experience difficult, emotionally laden situations and discover their capacity to resolve them well. Edwin Locke, Dean's Professor (Emeritus) of Leadership and Motivation at the R. H. Smith School of Business at the University of Maryland, isn't as convinced as others as to whether we yet know how to accurately measure emotional intelligence or if we realize the degree to which it is an influencing variable. Locke received his degree in industrial psychology in 1964, the zenith of behaviorism in the United States. He now writes for the Ayn Rand Institute, which is dedicated to the principles of objectivism, reason, and rational self-interest. He has studied many corporations and leaders from a different emotional intelligence angle. In one newspaper article that reviewed some of the hype on the subject, Locke spoke about his study of former General Electric CEO Jack Welch: "Welch was a tough customer, and I'm not sure I'd call him emotionally sensitive. But I think there's little question he was an excellent leader."[15] Locke suggests that good business leaders are not known primarily for their introspection, but rather for their real rational intelligence.

On the one hand, pundits declare that emotional or social intelligence is highly important. On the other hand, they declare that emotional intelligence is difficult to define and that rationality is highly important. We believe the answer lies in understanding the best of both views. The research on the collision of intellect and emotions has advanced considerably over the past twenty years, and there are many good scientific conclusions that basically back up our general experience.

By answering three questions, we can gain some insight into the connection between emotions and intellect and the effects of maturity. The first question is, *Can people eliminate emotions from their decision making, and should they do it if they can?* The qualified answer to this is no. Leading neurologist Antonio Damasio is one among many who have concluded that our brains simply do not have independent operating systems called intellect and emotions that we can flip between. All decisions are made through the cooperation of emotional and logical modes of thought.[16] It is true that being overly emotional does degrade our ability to reason well. However, it is also well documented that controlling or denying emotion too much also leads to degradation in decision making. It is important to understand this, because the best decisions are made when we are working under more normal states rather than under heightened, emotional states. It is scientifically unsound to conclude that good decisions are the result of pure intellect and that bad decisions stem from our emotions being out of whack. Rational judgment is best observed when intellectual processes are robust and emotional states are in healthy, normal condition.

The second question we can examine to help us learn about the relationship between emotions, intelligence, and maturity has to do with emotional stability: *Do unpredictable emotional states influence leadership quality?* The answer is yes. Unpredictable or highly variable emotional states lead to distrust, and this of course erodes the effects of leadership. Even tough-minded bosses like Jack Welch can have positive leadership effects when their basic emotional responses and demeanors are relatively stable and when followers have a basis upon which to accurately predict the leader's emotional reaction to situations. This does not imply that command-and-control-oriented, insensitive—even, perhaps, demeaning—bosses are the best candidates for the leadership hall of fame, but people can work for leaders with these qualities. Such qualities do not necessarily produce the best results or working climate, but followers are able to work when they can predict emotional climates, even when those climates are harsh.

The third question concerns developing emotional maturity: *Can a person deliberately develop emotional maturity?* The answer is yes, but the one-hundred-thousand-Euro follow-up question is, *How?* Life experiences in general provide some of the answers to that question. Developing long-term friendships and stable social groups provide others. Even people who are born with various neurological challenges to emotional intelligence can learn greater emotional control, but the effort required is significant and nearly always requires expert help. For example, Asperger syndrome is a clinical variety of autism marked by "an inability to understand how to interact socially. Typical features of the syndrome also may include clumsy and uncoordinated motor movements, social impairment with extreme egocentricity, limited interests and unusual preoccupations, repetitive routines or rituals, speech and language peculiarities, and non-verbal communication problems. People with Asperger syndrome ('Aspies' as many call themselves) generally have few facial expressions apart from anger or misery."[17] This syndrome has a wide range of effects, and there is a lot of debate among high-tech companies as to how many high-IQ technologists may have mild forms of this condition. Steven Gutstein, codirector of the Houston-based Connections Center for Family and Personal Development, believes that people with various forms of autism can learn greater emotional intelligence through some hard work of a special nature, but notes that only 12 percent of adults with Asperger syndrome hold jobs.[18]

Organizational Authenticity

ON JUNE 1, 2006, Forbes.com named the Hyundai Azera the best luxury car for a non-luxury price, ranked behind Toyota's Avalon and Buick's Lucerne. Over the previous three years, this South Korean automotive manufacturer had been experiencing an amazing growth rate and was working to become ranked as one of the top five automakers in the world. Sales were sky-high, business periodicals were bullish on the company's fortunes, and it appeared that the days of "Hyundai who?" were history. Yet behind the scenes, several organizational issues were brewing that were causing cracks and strains. It seemed American managers could never please their Korean superiors, and the North American management staff was in constant turnover. Then, early in 2006, the news broke that both the chairman of Hyundai Motors, Chung Mong-koo, and his son, Kia Motors president Chung Eui-sun, were under investigation for their roles in scandals involving political slush funds and the misuse of company money, which may have involved bribery. When this news got out, per-share stock prices that had been hovering in the high nineties began falling, and as of June 2006, the same month that Forbes.com gave the Azera credit for its position in the marketplace, stock was trading in the mid-fifties. Like many stories involving senior managers' wrongful, incompetent, or even indecent behavior, the whole story may never be known. But in the Hyundai Motors case, the face-losing events of arrest and prosecution were swiftly followed by trials and imprisonments. Chung Mong-koo was sentenced to three years in jail on February 5, 2007.

When Kenneth Lay, the former CEO of Enron, died on July 5, 2006, his passing reminded many of another authenticity breach. Enron has been for many the vilest stain of corporate corruption experienced across a season of scandal. Despite the dreadful impact of the company's collapse upon many employees and other shareholders, Lay maintained his position that "Enron's collapse was due to a 'conspiracy' waged by short sellers, a handful of rogue executives whose activities were unknown to him, and the news media."[19] The editors of *The Economist* dubbed him "the face of America's turn-of-the-century corporate crime wave."[20]

The temptation to behave unethically confronts leaders regularly. When leaders decide to act unethically and the breach is discovered, they must provide others with a defense. The most common of these defenses are for leaders to simply distance themselves from the act, find someone else to blame, try to reframe or explain the action as a good thing, or use the "ends justified the means" explanation.[21]

These stories of Chung Mong-koo and Kenneth Lay serve as illustrations of how the failure of senior leaders is seen as a failure of the organization. And although the scale of senior management deceit can be large enough to kill an organization, normally it does not do so. Despite the effects of some of the senior leaders' errant behavior, analysts, shareholders, suppliers, and consumers can generally maintain a perspective that the organization isn't all bad just because one of the senior members is. Hyundai's stock and future may be rocky at the moment, but this can be attributed more to the traditional family-oriented South Korean business structure than to any irreparable harm done to the basic trust and distinction the company has acquired over the past decade. Current labor issues, if not resolved, may have more impact than Chung Mong-koo. But even as such issues have erupted, prominent outsiders nevertheless recognize the basic quality offering of the Azera.

Fundamentally all stakeholders—such as employees, customers, investors, suppliers, and the public at large—consider not only the exterior behaviors of organizations, but evaluate the interior motives and intentions as well. When bad deeds or unfortunate mishaps occur, it is easier in some way to point to a specific senior manager, especially a CEO or other top official, as the individual manager who serves as a symbolic proxy for the corporation. But it is the corporation's authenticity that is being tested, even in cases when stakeholders are making a judgment between a person and an institution. While it is true that a person can have a poor interaction with any organizational associate and mentally proclaim that "XYZ organization doesn't care about its customers," this simplified thinking can often be overcome by a later, more positive interaction with either the same or a different organizational representative.

But certain kinds of large-scale fraud, neglect, deception, conflict, or disaster can bring the organization as a whole into focus in the minds of stakeholders. During these times, the interior intentions of the organization may never be forgiven, regardless of what exterior behavioral correction is made.

Contemporary Outcomes for Organizational Authenticity

IT IS easy to heap insults upon infamously guilty liars and cheaters. Yet there is some evidence that it is not just the headline-grabbing cases of corporate corruption that create difficulties. In many cases the lackluster performance of mediocre CEOS leads to organizational stagnation, a waning of respect or regard for organizational identity or integrity, and an overall lack of organizational distinction. And part of this mediocrity appears to stem from the view of an organization as a *mechanism* rather than an *organism*. We are passionate capitalists, yet we believe the default statement that the primary purpose of any for-profit enterprise is to maximize shareholder return is not only sterile and simplistic, but it also does not resemble the real-world situation of any corporation.

The three contemporary critical outcomes that dominate organizational authenticity discussions are:

PERVASIVE CORPORATE VALUES

TRUSTED BRAND

DISTINCTION

Pervasive Corporate Values

WHETHER your company used to convincingly and visibly conduct their day-to-day affairs according to a defined set of guiding principles or simply had laminated versions of lofty sounding ideas that hung in the hallways and were conspicuously ignored before the last downturn, it would be hard to imagine that this is your current state of affairs. The debacles of the early part of this millennium have already become historic in the annals of corporate values. Recounting the market losses, personal devastation, or lingering shame of those companies whose leaders acted lawlessly or unethically is redundant. Equally redundant is reviewing the large case selections of companies that acted upon stated values and won the admiration of business and consumer communities around the world.

The issue today isn't whether or not corporate values have value, but rather the extent to which leaders create systems that promote, instill, and to a certain degree measure whether or not decisions and actions reflect the principles. This focus on "principles in action" needs to be pervasive, and individual leadership example alone, although admirable and necessary, is insufficient to ensure and maintain ethical postures for all associates of an enterprise. Two questions nearly always arise when discussing the deployment of corporate values:

- *How should we deploy corporate values?*

- *Do they make business sense?*

These two questions have been debated and answered adequately by many business authors and research groups. To learn more about corporate values deployment, we would suggest investigating any of the practices used by Johnson & Johnson (US), Marks & Spencers (UK), Rio Tinto (Australia), Norsk Hydro (Norway), Cemex (Mexico), BNP Paribas (France), or any other values-based organization that is held in high regard.

As far as the issue of corporate values making business sense, the research literature for this is long and hard won. International Business Ethics, an organization that sponsors research and provides training on the practical side of business ethics, cites a study by researchers Simon Webley and Elise More, who examined financial performance data for a significant portion of the Financial Times Stock Exchange 350 from 1997 to 2001. The two researchers examined companies with codes of ethics/principles/conduct that had been in place for five years or more versus those companies that explicitly said they did not have such codes. Among their findings, they concluded the following:

- Companies with ethics codes generated significantly greater economic value added and market value added during 1997 to 2000 than those without codes.

- Companies with codes experienced less P/E ratio volatility during the four-year period than those without codes.[22]

Trusted Brand

AS A consumer, do you consider yourself a guileless dupe—an uninformed automaton who slavishly responds to the most interesting advertising that compels you to purchase a product? Or do you consider yourself someone who, while exhibiting certain levels of brand loyalty, is equipped to examine the usefulness of any product or service, and even in the case of extreme brand loyalty refuses to accept shoddy treatment, misrepresentation, or outright fraud? So how do you think your customers think?

Steve Yastrow suggests that much of modern branding "regards the customer as a passive participant to whom the brand is unveiled after its creation. By the time the customer gets involved, according to this model of branding, the brand is complete. The brand is assumed to be iconic and immutable, much like a statue of a dead general, which is designed in the artist's studio, cast by a skilled craftsman, and then unveiled and displayed in the town square in hopes of impressing everyone as they go by."[23]

Brand is intimately linked with authentic corporate behavior in the minds of customers, suppliers, and partners, but this is not necessarily so in the minds of senior executives—a dismaying, even if typically true, condition. Mergers and acquisitions were up 38 percent in 2005 over 2004 to a total near $2.7 trillion. By the end of 2006 the total was over $3.0 trillion. By mid-2007 Rob Brown, chief investment officer of Genworth Financial Asset Management, suggested the primary driver of thebull market is "vast and beyond belief" levels of M&A, buyout and stock buyback activity. Yet, "in many cases, the corporate brand strategy receives serious attention only after a deal is approved and the merger announced."[24] It seems many senior executives are motivated by operational, financial, or market share opportunities rather than by building a stronger brand—an authentic corporate position that people can trust and rely upon beyond any senior executives' tenure.

Corporate brand identity, let alone strategy, often seems to be a secondary consideration when M&A deliberations take place—except in the cases of those companies where authentic corporate behavior is an established norm and is seen as at least as important as financial performance. In simplistic terms, it is almost as if two single parents with children decide to get married by only considering the financial and operational aspects of what their combined union might be, and then informing the children and other close relatives about the decision after a wedding date has been set. Then the betrothed begin dealing with how their children view the decision and how it will affect their lives.

Given our previous discussion, it seems that growth and financial performance often drive organizational decision making to a greater degree than do considerations of organizational authenticity.

Distinction

TOM PETERS is a virtuoso when it comes to delivering rants about distinction. He scours the world's output of exclamations about how to become distinct, why distinction counts, and how it serves survivability. He was, perhaps, the person who coined the term "distinct or extinct."

Distinction comes in many forms. Having an offering that no one else has confers distinction (think pharmaceutical company patents). Difficult-to-replicate processes, like those offered through Dell, Inc., can create distinction. Attention to the total customer experience can bring significant distinction, as Apple often proves. Having operationally efficient processes combined with a distinct attitude toward the service provided can create distinction. Starbucks is a fine example of this. Not following the lead of the industry giant but instead staying true to core values and offering products of a different nature can create distinction and increase profits. Comparing and contrasting Nike with New Balance yields some thoughts about distinction. Combining tradition-bound values and sentiment with modern-day merchandising can refresh a brand and invoke a new sense of distinction, as in the case of Selfridges & Co. department stores. Creating a business proposition and market for a service that, while admirable, is not a huge wealth-generating machine can create a social distinction, such as that created by Grameen Bank through its microcredit system.

Distinction can be a faddish veneer or a deeper, more values-driven proposition. The first method requires a great amount of sensitivity to the fickle fate of fads and the fractionalization of global audiences. The second method can be slow to change and therefore not seem to change during tumultuous times. Either extreme offers an organizational leader an opportunity to create an organization that is as recognizable as any famous person. In fact, great organizational leaders work much harder on the distinction processes that drive their organization's success than upon those that garner personal acclaim.

Additional Thoughts on Authenticity

"THERE are two levers for moving men—interest and fear," Napoleon Bonaparte is reported to have said.[25] Bonaparte anticipated modern psychology's understanding of the basic fight-or-flight neural wiring of normally functioning humans. We fight for our interests if we determine that doing so is possible, or we retreat from danger. Fear and inspiration are primal drivers of these reactions.

The idea that leaders can use fear rather than interest—or inspiration if you like that idea better—as their key motivational method has been debated for as long as leadership has been studied. In the appendix to this book you can find several additional sources, quotes, and narratives about the development of and resistance to authenticity. The groundwork for this discussion is well laid, even though most energetic leaders still debate the issues.

Can leaders produce results through methods other than enlightened leadership? In other words, can an authentically power-hungry, narcissistic, or hard-minded, command-and-control-oriented person gain power over resources, then marshal those resources toward preconceived goals and gain results? You bet.

It's easy to argue the case when people like Bill Gates, Larry Ellison, Hank Greenberg, Jack Welch (remember Neutron Jack?), Andy Grove, and other very successful businesspeople are used as examples. All of these empire builders have shown characteristics of both inspirational and power-driven authentic behavior, yet all of them have been criticized at some point along the way for their heavy-handed guidance, and in one or two cases for their ruthlessness. And the economic-wealth creation is inarguable. There are also people whose intentions were nobler than economic advancement (even though economic health is a worthy goal for a person or society) who can also be viewed askance. Martin Luther King Jr., Mahatma Gandhi, and Mother Teresa all had their detractors. Authenticity as an idea by itself does not necessarily imply virtue over vice. When it comes to leadership, however, it is important to ask, *Which is the more sustainable force over time—fear or inspiration?*

Manfred Kets de Vries addressed this issue when he was interviewed for an article in the *Harvard Business Review*. He spoke about fear as an authentic part of some leaders, regardless of their position:

> The fact is that even scant authority can get away with murder, both literally and figuratively. Indeed, I would say that some organizations are so political and unsafe that they resemble concentration camps. Everyone kowtows to authority out of tremendous fear. And you can see why. I once met an executive who told me, "Every day when I walk

into the office, I can make the lives of 10,000 people completely miserable by doing very, very little." His company was probably not a very healthy workplace. Why wouldn't he say, "By doing very, very little, I can make the lives of 10,000 people much easier."[26]

Consider the idea of authenticity in terms of individual and organizational marque, and the issue becomes more poignant. The authentically power-based but gifted leader faces eventual diminishing returns, even though the diminishment may not occur for a long time and the run-up of wealth may be considerable. Fear ultimately leads to distrust, and lack of trust is the number one cause of executive derailment. The literature on emotional intelligence demonstrates that autocratic or command-oriented methods, even when effective during times of crisis, produce the least results over time. What effects do these leaders who are authentic power mongers have upon the organizational marque of a company after the riches have been made but the diminishment begins?

The answer to this question varies depending upon case examination, but the research community agrees that leaders who are authentically power-centered, command-and-control-driven, fear-based individuals leave behind more problems than they create sustainable wealth. If their enterprises are inherited by authentic leaders who possess the talents of inspiration rather than fear, then the wealth creation has a chance. The talented Bonaparte, who once said, "A leader is a dealer in hope," also remarked, "I love power. But it is as an artist that I love it. I love it as a musician loves his violin, to draw out its sounds and chords and harmonies."[27]

While some may regard Bonaparte as an artistic master of how to use fear and inspiration, each individual leader must authentically decide which mix of fear and inspiration works best for him or her. Organizations and organizational leaders face the same authenticity dilemma. Do their actions and interactions with the ecosystem create fear or inspiration, disgust or admiration, a fallout or a following? Each individual leader must wrestle with his or her own tolerance for tyranny and their own appetite as a tyrant within their own mind and soul.

3 Navigation

IMAGINE this.

You are the head of a new management team brought in to take over a very tough situation. The outgoing management team had brokered an unpopular takeover some time ago, and their programs and organizational structure decisions were aimed at nullifying or eradicating prior, popular cultural norms. The outgoing management team's performance was dismal: they are leaving you with debt and no liquidity, outdated plants and offices, and a workforce that has lost the ability to trust management. The expression "fog of battle" is sometimes used by business leaders to describe the complexity of making forward movement during the fluid, uncertain conditions of the commercial marketplace. But in our imaginary scenario the situation strikes you far more as the fog of despair—beyond apathy or disengagement; some of these workers have nearly lost their will to care. Others want—even demand—change, but the pent-up frustration has led to an unreasonable demand on time frames. And to top off the situation, as the proposed president of the replacement management group, you have a prison record as a political troublemaker and were handpicked by the outgoing, inept, and disliked administration to head up this new era.

Every question you formulate about how to get started spawns a dozen more questions. The barriers to making any movement at all seem insurmountable. Time is short. Strikes loom and the atmosphere is toxic. The expectations of the associates and their families have been placed into your hands, and they weigh more heavily than you had expected. Both you and they wonder if the effort is worth it anymore. You sought the job, but now wonder if the job is more difficult than you can handle. The most pressing question is this: How can you inspire these people to believe that there is a destination worth striving for and that there is a way forward?

This was the situation faced by Václav Havel, the last president of Czechoslovakia and first president of the Czech Republic during the early days of modern Europe's post-Soviet transformation. During the Velvet Revolution, 1988 to 1995, many Soviet-controlled regions acquired new constitutions and established independent nations. The Czech Republic and Slovakia were two such nations, formed from the dissolution of Czechoslovakia.

Václav Havel was born in 1936, and his early developmental years were bolstered by family wealth, intellectual stimulation, and traditional values. He witnessed World War II as a boy through tradition-bound values and watched his family's indignation, humiliation, and eventual destruction as it and the country were dismantled. At the age of twelve, he saw a Moscow-backed Communist political coup turn his country into a de facto Soviet state. His family was declared an enemy of that state, and their property was confiscated. Václav's full-time education was suspended at the elementary level. He started work during the day as a laboratory technician and finished high school at night. In college he studied economics, because his applications to liberal arts schools were rejected. He persisted in developing his natural talents, however, and studied drama through correspondence and eventually earned a degree. Interlaced with his obligatory military service, he worked as a stagehand and in a brewery for a number of years. Eventually, his humanitarian family background and dissatisfaction with Communism propelled him into political dissent. He wrote politically oriented plays, letters, and essays during the same time and became one of the cofounders of the Committee for the Defense of the Unjustly Prosecuted. He was labeled a subversive for his outspoken civic views and was jailed three times, spending a total of nearly five years in prison.

In 1979 Václav Havel's essay "The Power of the Powerless" resounded throughout Eastern Europe. Zbygniew Bujak, a Solidarity activist, is reported to have said the following about Havel's words:

> This essay reached us in the Ursus factory in 1979 at a point when we felt we were at the end of the road. We had been speaking on the shop floor, talking to people, participating in public meetings, trying to speak the truth about the factory, the country, and politics. There came a moment when people thought we were crazy. Why were we doing this? Why were we taking such risks? Not seeing any immediate and

tangible results, we began to doubt the purposefulness of what we were doing. Shouldn't we be coming up with other methods, other ways?

Then came the essay by Havel. Reading it gave us the theoretical underpinnings for our activity. It maintained our spirits; we did not give up, and a year later—in August 1980—it became clear that the party apparatus and the factory management were afraid of us. We mattered.[1]

The despair in Bujak's comments echoes the sentiments of others living throughout the Soviet satellite states.[2]

How did Havel approach the situation of a new Czech Republic? He lifted the fog of despair and replaced it with a glimmer of hope. His New Year's Day speech in 1991 was massively successful in restoring hope for a beleaguered people who thought, as many in converting countries or companies do, that the new progressive regime would right wrongs and economic prosperity would follow as an immediate consequence. While we recommend reading Havel's speech in its entirety to gather the full scope of his statements and the eloquence of his thoughts, below is an excerpt from the speech that showcases the basic metaphorical scaffolding he used to frame his remarks.

Dear fellow citizens,

There used to be a time when this country's president could have delivered the same New Year's Address he had given a year before, and nobody would have noticed. Fortunately, that time has passed.

Time and history have reentered our lives. The bleak skies of dullness and paralyzing inaction have cleared up. And we cannot help but be astonished at the range of possibilities emerging in a truly free political climate, and how it can always produce fresh surprises for us, in the good as well as the bad sense of the word.

Allow me to mention first all the unpleasant surprises the past year has brought us.

Primarily, it has become clear that the legacy of the past decades we have to cope with is even worse than we anticipated or could anticipate in the joyful atmosphere of those first weeks of freedom. New problems are emerging day by day, and we can see how interconnected they are, how long it takes to solve them, and how difficult it is to establish priorities.

> We knew that the house we had inherited was not in good shape. The stucco was falling off in places, the roof looked rather dubious, and we had doubts about some other things as well. After a year of examination, we have discovered to our distress that all the piping is rusted, the beams are rotten, the wiring is badly damaged. We know that the reconstruction already planned and anticipated will take much longer and be much more expensive than we originally believed.[3]

The house metaphor is both common and vividly rendered.

While this much of the passage seems gloomy, Havel continues to march through the very specific accomplishments of the first year: free elections and free speech were established, a constitution was adopted, religious life was restored, support and admiration from the free world was gained, economic reforms were set in motion, and the Soviet army departed. He helps citizens see that "much more has been accomplished in a single year than was done over the past forty-two years."[4]

It is a masterful, navigationally oriented oratory. And it completely complies with Howard Gardner's view that in order to change peoples' minds, a leader must "produce a shift in the individual's 'mental representations'—the particular way in which a person perceives, codes, retains, and accesses information."[5] These mental representations are not just about measuring the activity of movement, often called *execution*, but also about moving toward something so meaningful that it can alter your mental view.

People felt for the first time in their lives that they had been told the unvarnished truth—that the future would be bright only if they applied their own hearts, minds, and bodies to the task. And success has generally followed from that time for both the Czech Republic and Slovakia. The regions united in 1991 as Czechoslovakia but separated shortly thereafter, and Havel was quickly elected as the first president of the Czech Republic. A sense of navigation fueled by its most powerful companion, hope, was established, and Czech citizens aligned themselves to the task.

Vision, purpose, mission, and strategy at different times compete as synonyms for this labor of leadership. While everyone agrees that all of these ideas are important, at different times one or the other recedes or takes center stage in corporate debates. This oscillation points to the interdependent nature of purpose and path. The leader-as-navigator idea isn't just about creating a stimulating vision and laboriously delineating a strategy. It also involves the ongoing dynamics of affirming purpose and finding suitable paths that allow the community to live out that purpose. Vision and strategy are key elements of a coherent story that allows leaders to stimulate greater *alignment* as well as to update the coherent story as necessary *adaptations* to new realities occur. The labor of navigation concerns creating and maintaining alignment while constantly dealing with adaptive changes to social, political, industrial, technical, and consumer dynamics.

Individual Navigation—Alignment

DISCONTINUITIES included, all paths forward are connected to paths formerly trodden. All destinations are dreams until attained. All alignment occurs when the arc of time from past, present, and future creates a compelling story not just of where we are going and how we are going to get there, but also where we have been and what that has meant, and where we are today and what it will mean to continue the journey to this particular place. Various researchers write conclusively that goal clarity, vision stimulation, strategic thinking, contingency planning, purpose declaration, and other component parts of the future portion of navigation are the critical elements. We agree they are crucial; however, we do not believe that any single factor, past, present or future, is the key. The human mind does not consider the future independently from the past or the present. As John Gardner once put it, "Leaders act in the stream of history."[6]

Alignment is dynamic, not static, and therefore it is necessarily a never-ending process. Each action, each decision, each disruption causes a change to the stream, and every person updates his or her story about where the organization is going and why accordingly. If the destination and strategy are powerful enough, small deviations on a daily basis are absorbed and the overall coherency of where, how, when, and why go relatively undisturbed. But to overlook the cumulative effects of small changes may simply be navigational neglect, and in today's age this is commensurate to capsizing. Moreover, while general leadership and strategic skills are highly transferable from one place to another, among the many notable caveats to this general rule there is one that is particularly worth pointing out here: context.[7]

New to the situation or born to the situation, skilled leaders understand that context should never be underestimated when it comes to inspiring alignment. But what creates context? The fundamental tool that leaders possess to inspire a shared vision or affirm purpose is communication. Communication can set context and explain the ever-changing stream of history so that the members of a community will align their hopes, dreams, actions, and intent to a shared future.

We have found that the better navigators all use a basically similar communication process in their context-setting, alignment-seeking, and inspiration-producing declarations. The diagram that follows (Diagram 3) notes the four important points that a leader must consider when uniting the organization in a common cause.

Our ideas about the context-setting, stream-of-history-defining, coherent-story-making subject of alignment were largely developed from our field research. Recent neurological evidence suggests the underlying mechanisms at work. Joseph LeDoux, the Henry and Lucy Moses Professor of Science at New York University, asserts, "[O]ne of the main jobs of consciousness is to keep our life tied together into a coherent story, a self-concept. It does this by generating explanations of behavior on the basis of our self-image, memories of the past, expectations of the future, the present social situation, and the physical environment in which the behavior is produced."[8]

This coherent story, the one that each person concludes makes sense to them, is the one that sets context when it comes to navigation. It mixes past, present, and future together into a hologram of reality, upon which decisions are made, hopes are fueled, and actions are produced. On top of that, some mention of self-image and the current physical environment helps, according to LeDoux. This basic neurological science explains a great deal of the behavior observed in masterful leaders.

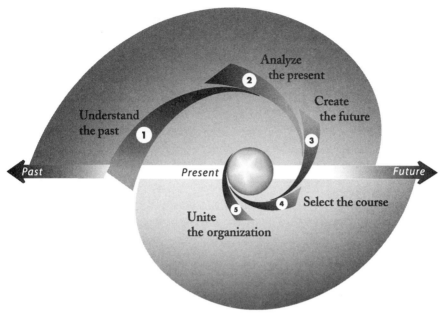

Past

Present

Future

Understand
the past ①

② Analyze
the present

Create
the future
③

④ Select the course

⑤ Unite
the organization

Diagram 3

Understand the Past

THE PAST is not fixed. It changes with the currents of perspective over time, emotional distance and diffusion, and the reinterpretation of events as details come into and out of review. Consider any important event from your childhood and think about how your perspective of this memory has changed over time. Any memory can be updated, altered, or reinforced when someone else who was there recalls information about the past or when someone who was not there can offer perspective on the story about the past. In fact, memory works by reconstructing past events from the flotsam and jetsam of the mind's neural net, not by accessing a digitally stored video and replaying it. Although some memories are vivid enough that the general details are recalled with reliable fidelity, the way we actually remember the past is by *reassembling* it, not by *replaying* it. This means that new data about the past or changed emotions about the past can cast new interpretations upon the meaning of the past. Recalling the past is not just a matter of enumerating facts, often numerical in nature and shifted by statistical or analytical processes, and then listing these facts in an indelible manner as if this undisputed evidence constitutes the whole of the past.

Leaders who seek alignment know that what the past means is a more powerful component to the coherent story than a list of dates, names, costs, revenues, and data infinitum. The key is *understanding the past*—what it means in the scope of the coherent story. As Kathleen Hall Jamieson, professor of communication and the director of the Annenberg Public Policy Center at the University of Pennsylvania, stated in one of her earliest works on modern communication, "Without understanding who we have been and what it has meant, it is difficult to reconceive where we are going or ought to go."[9]

During the city-state period of human history, part of a person's or family's political power was derived from linking lineage to former greatness or great deeds. In writing about the mist-enshrouded legends of Troy, Agamemnon, Achilles, and Helen, author Cathy Gere points out: "Appeals to the legendary past served as a way to secure control over tracts of land. If a ruling family could link itself in some way with the hero who had once inhabited a place, its claim to ownership of that locality was greatly enhanced."[10] If you doubt that this is pertinent today, listen to any modern political, business, or religious leader who is caught up in the numerous ideological conflicts that challenge modern times, and listen for how the claims to the past help lay claims to the present and future.

All organizations have history. But not all members of an organization have lived through the same history, which results in a wide variety of interpretations, stories, and myths concerning the past. Some of the more popular, repeated, or notable events within an organization become emblematic symbols of its past rights or wrongs, victories or defeats, or other defining moments. They serve as narrative evidence of what the company was at that time—its posture, brand image, competitiveness, and worth symbolically coded and generally understood by most associates regardless of their length of tenure. Some events are controversial, and the contestable interpretations of these events lead to a difference in the process of understanding the past. Ignoring the effect that history's stream has upon the ability to align organizational members is at best insensitive and at worst disastrous.

All of us tend to distort interpretations of the past. We often refer to hindsight as being twenty-twenty, yet significant research indicates it is not. We select preferred details of the past, blend them into a savory explanation that suits our tastes, and subsequently tend to refer to that particular version of past events unless we are prompted to reconsider. Repeated references to this same explanation reinforces our preferred version of the past, and over time it becomes so familiar, so sensible, that we begin to believe we could have predicted this outcome before its occurrence. This process of "past prediction" is known as *hindsight bias*. When we begin to believe that our explanation is the best or only one, we then begin to argue that our view is the inevitable version of history, our creeping determinism the result of not just blinding ourselves to other views, but of becoming convinced that our views are the only ones that make genuine sense. It is a process that bakes myths into hardened fact and indelibly links our current reality with the preferred interpretation of the past.

Hindsight bias and creeping determinism can limit our ability to understand and explain current events, which in turn can limit our vision of the future. To overcome this phenomenon, we have to revisit the past to see if our version really is the only or best one. Talking with others about their experience and knowledge of the past may open our minds to alternate explanations. Asking the question "What if my explanation is not exactly right?" can help us reimagine the past, for the purpose of enriching our sense of how we have arrived at the present and what our future possibilities might be.

In order to establish context, a leader must have as compelling a story about the past as he or she has vision for the bright and shining future. New courses can be set, but only if the leader can change the context for the entire story, including doing an honest examination of the past and connecting its truths to the realities of present and future. We think Havel's metaphor of inheriting a ruined house is an eloquent example that sets the stage for his comments about present circumstances and how the house will be repaired in the future.

Analyze the Present

MODERN businesses excel at analyzing the present. Huge amounts of time are spent looking over hourly, daily, weekly, and quarterly indicators of quality, market position, financial health, customer responsiveness, brand loyalty, and other inputs and outputs. The density of current activity can make people lose sight of the past and future. We may be so busy laying tarmac, measuring and painting highway stripes, and making sure the roadside reflectors meet regulatory guidelines that we forget where the road started or where it is going. Focusing too much on the present creates a behavioral myopia that can have difficult consequences.

Create the Future

"LEADERS conceive and articulate goals that lift people out of their petty preoccupations, carry them above the conflicts that tear a society apart and unite them in pursuit of objectives worthy of their best efforts."[11] John W. Gardner's thought strikes a chord with nearly all leaders. Uniting others to pursue objectives to the best of their abilities is often the driving force behind the ideas of operational excellence and flawless execution. These are the outputs. The inputs are conceiving and articulating worthy goals and lifting people above petty conflicts such as divisional infighting, functional squabbling, regional differences, and other silo barrier irritations that are such a natural feature of human behavior that leaders must regularly work to prevent them. Creating the future is the part of the coherent story that establishes why all the past victories and defeats and current struggles are worth any effort at all. Creating the future is not merely a statement of the obvious or a statement so generic that it could apply to any organization. It is that special statement that finishes the arc of history with a declaration of a better future, one that is worth the effort, one that especially applies to this time, this group, and this set of worthy endeavors. Overall, the past, present, and future convey the part of the coherent story we label *purpose*, which Nikos Mourkogiannis, senior executive adviser on leadership to Booz Allen Hamilton, suggests "gives the array of these actions coherence, not just at any given moment, but over time, and thus helps ensure that the firm does achieve a genuine specialisation, a genuine difference from its competitors."[12]

Most of the time purpose in for-profit organizations is related to some combination of excellence (premier class, most admired), innovation (most inventive, best design), or effectiveness (most profitable, most durable). Nonprofit organizations regularly add helpfulness to the list (most responsive to community needs, highest levels of service, greatest compassion).

Select the Course

DECLARING a purpose, vision, mission, preeminent goal, or other means of stimulating a mental image of the coherent story is incomplete without a way forward. Strategy and ideas about strategic thinking, strategic goals, and strategy as a science and art form dominate the literature and debate on the subject. Indeed, during the foggy period of the general economic downturn that occurred during the birth of the twenty-first century, many companies focused on survival and envied the great number of new businesses, business plans, and business forms that change produced. Some people have considered this as a type of Cambrian explosion period in business development that led to a huge number of new business design potentials, many of which subsequently died. But the ensuing period was different. While some people may support the idea that the business landscape is still undergoing massive change, the reality is that once general economic growth was reestablished, strategy reemerged from its survivalist limitations and placed itself center stage in many business leaders' minds. As one of the great authorities on strategy, Michael Porter, declared: "This is the moment to rediscover strategy, and an opportunity to scrape off the barnacles acquired during the last expansion. The essence of strategy is defining how a company is unique and how it will deliver distinctive value. Strategy is about aligning every activity to create an offering that cannot easily be emulated by competitors."[13]

We agree with the essentials of Porter's views. Strategy involves delivering a mix of value, aligning activities that support the coherent story, and creating a competitive position. There are many paths to the destination, and strategizing sorts through the various paths and selects those that are most favorable to the strengths and weaknesses of the firm. Communicating only this portion of the story invites fog, but so too does not communicating it clearly enough. Strategy alone does not constitute alignment, but it remains a crucial piece of the equation.

Continuing with the idea that times of greater change require active mutation and times of greater stability favor less mutation, we argue that some level of mutation is required at any time, and that strategy can never remain fixed over long periods of time. Overall goals can remain fixed; the plan for achieving them cannot. It is better to think of strategic thinking and strategy formation as an ongoing dynamic, which David C. Wilson and Paula Jarzabkowski describe as the "interplay between thinking and acting strategically. This interplay need not be continuous, nor need it be linear. Indeed oscillation between thinking and acting may be a more accurate term for describing how strategising emerges. Strategising goes beyond the map and its semiotics and examines the processes by which strategies are fashioned and lived in organisations."[14]

The nonlinear nature of strategy is generally an experienced and accepted fact in modern organizations. Strategic updates, a natural consequence of strategy shifts, lead to a tendency to communicate about this portion of the coherent story only. However, because strategy changes often require organizational adjustments in architecture, each one also provides potential for the coherent story to evolve and change. Periodic reinforcement of the entire coherent story is required, even if the only portion of the story that shifts is the strategy. Gary Hamel and C. K. Prahalad, in their seminal book, *Competing for the Future*, spotted the trend of overemphasizing strategy and underemphasizing other components of the coherent story.[15] This development is an understandable consequence of time-pressed, sensory-overloaded managers that requires conscious effort to resist.

Alignment is the crucial issue for individual navigation. As Dick Nettle, senior vice president at Bank of America, reminds us, "If you don't have alignment, then all you really have is adult day care."[16]

Contemporary Outcomes for Individual Navigation

Gaining directional clarity, maintaining commitment to this direction, and stimulating ongoing action toward it are contemporary as well as historical goals for leaders. In fact, some researchers have argued that such activities are axiomatic—foundational activities that define navigation. Unfortunately, at different times and places, organizations emphasize one of these three outcomes to the exclusion of the others and remain frustrated when the fog doesn't dissipate.

Other important topics have been reviewed and debated as to how to inspire vision, whether or not vision cocreation is better than one leader inspiring the rest with revealed vision, how a leader maintains personal inspiration, how far into the future visions should try to extend, and the enumeration of critical vision elements. All of these are worthy topics in their own right, but for the moment it appears the three most pressing topics are the following:

CRYSTAL-CLEAR DIRECTION

WIDESPREAD COMMITMENT

PURPOSEFUL ACTION

Crystal-Clear Direction

The effects of fog in world business affairs during the business downturn of the millennial period have been followed immediately by the blossoming of a wide variety of business models and new markets. Outsourcing as a cost-control craze continues to enjoy its moment for now, but Indian and Chinese businesspeople have shown that they are not willing to be low-cost providers forever. The pace of the change in the world scene produced an upturn fog that is as disconcerting as the downturn fog. Since the fog-induced period has persisted for several years, it is not remarkable that leaders, shareholders, and associates are desperately seeking clarity of direction. Add to the upturn dynamics a merger-manic business orientation, and it becomes easy to see why most people have defaulted to a (perhaps necessarily) myopic view of the direction of all businesses:

growth. Maximize your size and reach, since the world has suddenly tripled in size, and hope you get your share, and if you are IPO bound, get out at the top of the share price.

There is nothing wrong with growth, growth strategies, or maximizing earnings. Using these as the main components of the coherent story, however, produces exactly what we are seeing in the workforce today: widespread disengagement. People are glad there are jobs, and they work pretty hard, but they just don't believe in their companies anymore, because the coherent story isn't big enough. Despite the cry for a greater balance between work and life, people are seeking greater meaning from the work portion of the equation, and emphasizing the goals of growth and profits is insufficient to inspire them for long. The complaint is clarity; the cure is greater meaning. Apple usually gets it. Sir Richard Branson, in his variety of Virgin identities, usually gets it. Southwest Airlines usually gets it. FedEx usually gets it.

Widespread Commitment

It follows that commitment increases when meaning increases, not just clarity. Obtaining and maintaining commitment is not an easy task. The flies in the ointment today are overwork and loss of face-to-face contact. The e-mail glut is the most chronic complaint managers identify when it comes to having time to "inspire the troops." It is also on the list of top ten reasons that managers are often uninspired. The corollary to, if not the cause-effect companion of, e-mail glut is distance management. Far too many teams seldom visit one another in person, use conference-call times effectively, or know how to use modern information technology in its varied forms as a tool for spurring inspiration. Many team members and managers complain that the amount of face time with their managers is at an all-time low. Inspiration can take place without direct face-to-face contact; consider, for example, Martin Luther King Jr., Gandhi, or Mother Teresa. In business, however, inspiration requires more metrics than social or religious consciousness-raising does. It requires more of the measurable day-to-day progress that is often an automatic by-product of for-profit business than wider-spread human rights issues provide. The data is clear on this point: people become more accomplished when they are inspired.

Take, for example, the issues of clarity discussed above: growth and profit are the prime clarifiers. Add to this the idea that most of the interaction received from leaders is transactional in nature and delivered via e-mail's impersonal methodology, and then ask yourself why you are not getting and maintaining commitment.

The remedy lies in two areas. First, increase the quality of the face time and the inspirational energy the leader provides. Second, increase the quality of non-face-to-face correspondence.

Purposeful Action

Navigation is only an idea until the ship sets sail. It takes thousands of choreographed, energetic actions and behaviors from committed individuals to put navigation into action and move the company forward. What matters is that people behave in ways that move the company toward the destination, generally along intended strategic trajectories (although let's not entirely rule out serendipitous events). If the fog is too thick and malaise is widespread, how can any individual person know if any of his or her actions will result in a good outcome? This question falls in the easy-to-answer, difficult-to-do category. However, if the way forward is crystalline and inspiration is rampant, leaders may still have the same easy-to-answer, difficult-to-do problem if they lack sufficient resources or adequate business architecture. In this case, the problem isn't fog—it's traction.

Actions toward the goals and vision of the group are often only known to be purposeful, meaning that they gained the intended outcome, after the fact. Imagine being part of a rowing team. The coxswain's megaphone-amplified voice establishes a rhythm, the course is known, and each pull and stroke of an oarsman has immediate, ready-made feedback. Now imagine that the coxswain sends an e-mail that is received in a download of fifty or so e-mails that each rower reads at different times, and then half the rowers ask for more information before pulling a stroke, while the other half pull at widely varying times.

Inside most corporations the feedback loop is often arduous and arcane, and leaders-as-navigators must close the feedback loop. They must let the collective know that the energy expended and actions taken are successfully moving the organization toward its goal. The coherent story becomes a story in motion when leaders continue to update the story through purposeful action updates.

Organizational Navigation—Adaptation

"A DECADE ago, the possibility that Chinese companies would pose a serious competitive challenge to multinationals appeared improbable. It wasn't surprising, therefore, that, in 1995, just a few years after China's personal-computer market opened up to foreigners, *The Economist* predicted that by 2000, multinationals would have captured an 80% market share from their hapless Chinese competitors. And it appeared that this prediction would be on target, as multinationals like IBM, Hewlett-Packard and Compaq quickly won more than 50% of the market."[17]

It's another amazing technology story about how quickly local Chinese computer manufacturers adapted to the threat. By 2000, Lenovo, known at the time inside China as Legend, had captured 29 percent of the market and struggled against its two nearest Chinese competitors, who, combined, had 14 percent of the market at the turn of the century. The 80-percent-penetration prediction was never achieved by outsiders. By mid-2004 it had dropped from 50 percent to 20 percent. In early December 2004, Lenovo purchased IBM's PC hardware business, making it the third largest supplier in the world. One Lenovo official told the BBC at the time that the deal was a dream come true and a matter of national pride.[18]

It hasn't been a picnic for Lenovo. Dell slashed prices in 2005. Acer—the Taiwanese competitor that has all the looks of a scrappy pugilist who knows he may never make it to the big ring, but believes he could win if he did make it there—is coming on strong. And all competitors are scrambling to figure out how to approach India with PC sales. While China and the United States are still the main battlegrounds between Dell, HP, and Lenovo, India looms large, but with a twist. Consumers are unaccustomed to online purchasing in the world's largest democracy. "The Dell online purchasing model doesn't work," says Joseph Ho, an analyst with Daiwa Institute of Research in Hong Kong, in reference to Lenovo's potential advantage over its rivals in reaching India.[19]

Which was more adaptive? Lenovo thinking large enough to pursue the purchase of IBM? Or IBM considering its navigational posture and letting go of its PC marketplace to focus on mainframes and service? Arguments could be made for either position, and both represent what we call *navigational adaptation*.

Leader-as-navigator tasks change considerably as the individual leader now thinks and acts as an organizational leader. The main goal of the individual leader-as-navigator is to create and maintain alignment by creating a coherent story. The main goal of the organizational leader-as-navigator is to search for two basic kinds of stories—the evolution of the current story in its varied possibilities, and totally different stories. Organizational leaders not only search for stories, but they also try them on, see if they play out, and then select from the potential candidates the one that is most advantageous, most adaptive to changing environments. They must also prepare the organization for a story change, one that could be represented metaphorically by a simple change in a cast of characters or a significant shift in genre, from comedy to drama, action-adventure to tragedy.

"For a company to succeed over the long term it needs to master both adaptability and alignment," concludes Julian Birkinshaw and Cristina Gibson at the London School of Management.[20] Their work examines *ambidexterity* (a term that has been around for a while) and applies it to this issue of individual and organizational leader-as-navigator tension. They support the idea that alignment and adaptability should be considered complementary, not antagonistic or separate, activities, and that leaders at all levels should play a role in their communication and implementation.

Scenario planning, megatrend analysis (or gigatrends if you prefer *Wired* magazine's nomenclature), contingency planning, and other forms of sixty-thousand-foot-level prognostication are all forms of storytelling about the future. Collecting myriad forms of data on how the future may change and weaving them together in cogent and colorful ways is a form of disciplined daydreaming that is essential to the organizational navigator. A major problem these days is that organizations can literally create Alexandria library–sized sets of data on a regular basis, and sifting through the data leads to paralysis by analysis. The other extreme can occur, with each new potential story of the future seeming to confer such adaptive advantage that the organization finds itself a slave to constant reconceptualization and the new story's demand for reorganization. As Jeffery Immelt, CEO of General Electric, warns, "Organizations will tolerate iterating, but they will not tolerate permanent iterating."[21]

The first challenge for many organizational navigators is figuring out the rate of adaptation. To put it in evolutionary terms: "Active mutators in placid times tend to die off. They are selected against. Reluctant mutators in quickly changing times are also selected against."[22] Rate of change is the essential question. Few deny that most of the commercial world is in a rare period of rapid change, but the arguments swell as to whether the rate is increasing, decreasing, or remaining more or less the same. A great number of cases exist that demonstrate the success of new emergent businesses and the transformation of successful older business that have changed considerably. Equally persuasive, however, are the case studies of established companies that are changing at less rapid rates and seem to be securing an advantageous place in the commercial ecology. Globalization, as always, obscures the data, and its grandeur of scale often multiplies the effects of change out of proportion. Things aren't always moving as fast as it seems, and being blindsided is a more common occurrence than we like. The new millennial period is like hurricane tracking—determining how quickly conditions change helps determine whether a storm will increase to hurricane strength or decrease to mere sheets of tropical rain. Science and the art of experience combine forces in much the same way in navigating the future of an organization.

The second challenge is not detecting what adaptations to make or the rate of making them, but implementing the change. Generally speaking, the difficulty in change management begins with ineffective communication—the new coherent story needs time to be told persuasively and allowed some absorption time. Leaders may use the "turning a battleship on a dime" rhetorical imagery, but even the most able captains of the most advanced navies have yet to pull that off. In fact, a slightly slower, more gracefully executed turn can often produce greater advantage than ninety-degree pivots.

As much as we try to create data sensors of every kind from focus groups to Web crawlers and then develop ever more sophisticated algorithms and analytical engines to grind, pulp, and mold the collected data into a provable set of probabilities, each with its own believable story (with an acceptable margin of error), we must nevertheless face the truth: adaptation activities are as much art as science. The organizational navigator needs to study business like an anthropologist, rely on data like a physicist, contemplate like a poet, and communicate like an evangelist. Adapting to a new story, even when the story is demonstrably validated, requires faith in the adjustments made.

Contemporary Outcomes for Organizational Navigation

To ENABLE the organizational leader-as-navigator to do his or her job well, the following three contemporary outcomes have gained center-stage attention with many business leaders.

SCANNING SYSTEMS

OPPORTUNISTIC BIAS

PREMEDITATED AGILITY

Various experts provide insight into each of these three areas. Developing increasingly greater ability to scan the horizon, access and process emergent data, and turn this data into informed action is the central issue for scanning systems. Having a bias for action is a perennial, it seems—the idea that business must act upon opportunities earlier than competitors has become a staple in business thinking. Agility is a somewhat newer idea, and we've added the thought that to be agile requires a form of premeditation.

Scanning Systems

BETWEEN 2000 and 2005 Malcolm Gladwell underwent a transformation that is nearly every writer's dream. His reputation as a writer went from obscure to mainstream to idol, and eventually he was dubbed the "Accidental Guru."[23] His books, *The Tipping Point* and *Blink*, continue to enjoy a wide following, and like many well-researched business or science books, the basic ideas have passed into common vernacular, but often the difficult ideas behind the memorable phrase have not. We hear the words "tipping point" used as a mandate to keep our eyes and ears open to the earliest possible detection of a new trend, a new idea, the butterfly-wing beat that will change the world. Businesses set up various methods of scanning the environment for these signals, investing loads of money with the hope that they will recognize the signal when it arrives. Today the activity associated with finding tipping points is a hot topic in corporate circles.

What is often forgotten is the point that Gladwell raises toward the very end of his book:

> The theory of Tipping Points requires, however, that we reframe the way we think about the world. I have spent a lot of time, in this book, talking about the idiosyncrasies of the way we relate to new information and to each other. We have trouble estimating dramatic, exponential change. We cannot conceive that a piece of paper folded over 50 times could reach the sun. There are abrupt limits to the number of cognitive categories we can make and the number of people we can truly love and the number of acquaintances we can truly know. We throw up our hands at a problem phrased in an abstract way, but have no difficulty at all solving the same problem rephrased as a social dilemma. All of these things are expressions of the peculiarities of the human mind and heart, a refutation of the notion that the way we function and communicate and process information is straightforward and transparent. It is not. It is messy and opaque.[24]

We posit that scanning systems are only as good as our ability to reframe how we think about the world. Detection is the first part of scanning systems, and leaders must continually invest in the newest and most inventive means for doing so. But developing the ability to single out specific butterflies and count wing beats is useless unless it is accompanied by the ability to rethink, reframe, reconsider, and reimagine what the beats mean.

Leaders would be wise to invest in the richness of data that Internet traffic and activity provide. Blogs are the rage of the moment (although it remains to be seen how they will evolve over time), along with the usual social interactions known as focus groups, which are often helpful sources of information. And as critical as it is for individual leaders to not consume processed and packaged information, it is equally essential for them to gain direct experiences of their own. Everyday reflection upon our direct experience can be just as informative as scanning systems in assessing potential adaptations if we are willing to think about the world differently.

Opportunistic Bias

"READY, fire, aim!" has become such a standard business idea since it was first introduced by Tom Peters in his seminal work, *In Search of Excellence*, that even Peters no longer uses the phrase. In his usual exclamatory style, he has had to amp up his own idea with the more recent admonition of "Fire! Fire! Fire!" What all this urgency is conveying is the importance of having a bias for opportunity. It doesn't mean necessarily jumping in heedlessly (although some pundits do encourage that), but it definitely means taking more risks than not, even experimenting in marketplaces that already seem saturated and dominated by giant competitors.

Robert Greenberg is an entrepreneur who is dedicated to taking advantage of opportunity. He has started many a venture, including earning $3 million by selling shoelaces promoting the megahit movie *E.T.* The license to sell the laces cost him a reported $10,000.[25] Shortly after the *E.T.* project, he noticed his daughter's junior high school friends were wearing boys' high-top athletic shoes, and something clicked. The L.A. Gear enterprise story, while it ultimately failed, is one of opportunistic bias. Greenberg had been experimenting with a canvas workout shoe at the time and introduced girls' high-tops in pink. Later he added rhinestones and other styling details that allowed him to soar into the young girls' fashion accessory market. Sales went from $11 million to more than $800 million in an amazing five years. Although a series of unfortunate miscalculations ended the company, Greenberg quickly bounced back with Skechers, another company that takes an aggressively opportunistic look at a market dominated by Nike, changes styles quickly, and launches new fashion ideas in both footwear and now athletic clothing. Skechers made *BusinessWeek*'s top ten hot growth companies in 2000, 2001, and 2002. What Greenberg may have failed to see during his L.A. Gear days, he appears to have capitalized on with his new enterprise.

Greenberg is not competing directly against Nike in the performance shoe category; rather, his opportunistic bias has led him to see the market for fashion footwear. In 2005 fashion footwear sales were up 11.3 percent, while performance shoe growth grew at a steady rate of 2.5 percent. Marshall Cohen, chief industry analyst for market researcher NPD Group, reported that footwear "became a signature item. This year was the year that everybody—and I mean everybody—looked at their shoes."[26]

Although Greenberg's bias to invest in opportunity is perhaps a classic trait in an entrepreneur who was once described in a *Forbes* article as a "gregarious, diminutive man with a deep California tan, a thick Beantown accent, and an overdeveloped sense of showmanship,"[27] this very kind of appetite for taking on opportunities is currently one of the hottest ideas in leadership development.

Premeditated Agility

THIS seemingly oxymoronic idea isn't meant to convey a conundrum. Simply stated, premeditated agility means a consciously built-in ability to make adaptive changes ahead of time. Like many athletes who work their muscles and coordination in a variety of ways or consider nutrition to be an important component to maintaining their competitive edge so that they are premeditatedly agile, so too can companies engage in methods that allow them to adapt to change more easily.

The most *conservative*, though not necessarily *common*, method of maintaining a premeditated agility is financial liquidity. Much speculation is placed on Microsoft's continuous buildup and retention of cash, even with generous dividend payments in recent times. This company's attitude has always been that it could go out of business, meaning it could lose its adaptive ability to survive, in two years, and the company's cash coffers buffer this possibility. Southwest Airlines' cash retention strategy has helped it survive the United States airline industry downturn better than most. Plenty of counterexamples are available to any business student.

On the other hand, the most *common*, though not necessarily *conservative*, method of obtaining premeditated agility is through remaining innovative. We will explore this idea more in chapter 4, on architecture, where its role is more central, but it is worth noting here that retaining an innovative bias helps condition a company for agile moves. At one end of the innovative continuum is to constantly experiment in known arenas of expertise to further refine existing processes, services, or products, or to produce corollary processes, services, or products. At the other end is experimentation in foreign or even unknown ways that might significantly alter the course of a company.

The most unusual—and as a consequence the riskiest and sometimes most controversial—course is total reinvention. A commonly recited example is the Nokia story.[28] The United States parallel to Nokia might be considered Motorola, as it grew from a series of failed business launches by Paul Galvin into a successful manufacturer of radios that worked inside of early automobiles (Motorola is a coined word—"Motorcar" plus "Victrola"). These examples do represent adaptation in motion during an earlier, more chaotic time (consider that electricity was still a novelty during the period of Nokia's wood pulp mill and the first cars). While some might argue that these two companies' stories serve as examples of adaptation, they really don't represent "total reinvention." In the absolute sense this is true, but not many companies have pulled off even this level of adaptation. Both Nokia and Motorola made forays into arenas they later abandoned (televisions, for example), but each has survived as a business by adapting to new environments in very volatile industries.

Additional Thoughts on Navigation

IF WE agree that the coherent story is a necessary feature of human consciousness in general, and that the central most coherent story a business leader must provide is an understanding of a company's existence over time, especially its future destination and path forward, then several questions can be posed for the leader-as-navigator. We have chosen to examine three out of a number of knotty questions our clients often pose.

- *If economic viability or wealth creation is the important, sustaining vision for any company, thereby making all company destinations essentially the same, then does strategy take center stage in the coherent movie?*

- *What is the relationship between navigation and prediction?*

- *Is longevity an important, vital, necessary goal for an organization?*

Strategy Takes Center Stage

THE HYPER-COMMERCIAL age in which we live has seen classical and even modern strategic methods come under fire. From pronouncements that strategic planning is dead to sightings of its phoenix-like resurrection, all companies are furiously engaged in a wide range of strategic experimentation. Some researchers suggest, "[T]he strategy field is like a garden in which there are thousands of flowers blooming without any manicuring or tending to the garden. The problems created by this lack of 'pruning' permeate the meaning, methodology, and research methods in strategic management."[29]

While the flower metaphor is apt to describe what is happening in the field of strategy development—lots of variety, but little attention to the garden—a shift in metaphor answers the question regarding "strategy as center stage" a bit more precisely.[30] The search for better strategy is as it has always been—the search for the perfect lever. In fact the word *leverage* in its technical and casual business sense has to do with how to get more return out of a system by using different types of levers. While leverage often conjures the mental image of Archimedes standing at the end of a long pole somewhere outside the moon's orbit, pushing downward to move the earth, three more common tools can explain the three kinds of leverage most strategies seek to employ.

A crowbar is considered a first-class lever, because it literally changes the direction of a force. The fulcrum is between the effort being applied by your arms, shoulders, and hands and the force you want to move—a crate top, a door, or some other object. Strategies that attempt to change the direction of things are like crowbars.

Take two opposing forces—globalization and commoditization, say—and try to get one to move the other. This is a crowbar strategy. Dell is applying force on commoditization to move globalization—in other words, to dominate a global market with its crowbar of commodity execution. Dell has made this strategy work well for quite a long time, though current debates exist as to whether the crowbar strategy will continue to work.

A wheelbarrow is considered a second-class lever, with the wheel as the fulcrum. This lever works by applying force at one end and moving a resistance from one place to another. Using the wheelbarrow allows you to move more of something for the same force expended. In other words, you can carry more with a wheelbarrow than you can carry without it. This is essentially the outsourcing "strategy" that has gripped the world for the past decade. Since *near-sourcing* has become a new word in the business lexicon, it appears the wheelbarrow strategy is being reconsidered.

The third class of levers can be illustrated by a rake. The fulcrum of a rake is your hand at the top end of the rake; your other hand applies the force in the center of the rake, and the grass or leaves being raked are the force being moved. This is like most Internet strategies. By applying the same amount of force, the distance things can be moved can be increased. The same amount of effort applied can rake things in from a longer distance.

Each and every one of these strategies has taken center stage for business leaders at one time or another. We do not argue that the search for leverage is incorrect, but for many companies focusing too much on strategy has led to degradation in the coherent story: analysts wonder what business Dell is really in, customers wonder what happened to the promise of customer service as a result of the inept outsourcing many companies are now relying upon (try getting any call center rep to explain your cell phone bill), and many Internet companies don't rake in enough business to sustain themselves. The myopia that comes from putting these strategies at center stage constrains the coherent story, supplying it with insufficient meaning for constituents inside or outside the company to understand what the company is, why it exists, and how it will adapt in the future.

Navigation and Prediction

AN OLD argument exists among many political, social, business, and religious leaders as to whether or not individuals or groups would alter their path if they could accurately predict the future. For individuals, it seems it typically takes a crisis to produce a fundamental change in behavior—that is, it takes quite a bit of tension to alter a person's course of action. Even when smokers and drinkers are warned, they engage in somewhat risky behavior. Some people argue that the same is true for an organization. Sometimes it seems it takes quite a lot of pain for an organization to change. Even when its predictive abilities are acute, will an organization change?

From scenario planning, to better algorithms, to the use of prediction markets, a wide variety of new techniques and technologies are being employed to increase our ability to pierce the fog of uncertainty and lay greater claim to knowing what will happen in the future. The problem with most algorithms is that they are often hotly debated by experts or educated practitioners as to their inherent application to a particular problem. For example, in the CBS television series *NUMB3RS*, well-versed and intelligent mathematicians apply a wide range of algorithms to solve criminal cases. It's entertaining, but often short on the realities of data collection or number crunching.

Closer to current practice among businesses are prediction markets. Prediction markets ask employees to participate in a marketplace type of simulation in which they attempt to guess the outcomes of everything from which new features Yahoo! should supply to its users to the prices and volumes of product sales for everything from software to steel. The early evidence shows that prediction markets can help in some cases, but generally the wisdom of crowds seems to work only marginally better than other methods. Plus it tends to fail most often when applied to predicting future product prices.

In a sense, the prediction market method uses some sophisticated algorithms that rely upon information that is processed in a distributed network of sophisticated computers—namely, human brains. The success of the prediction market software is inherently linked to the level of participation by the employee group and the quality of their brain processing. If they are savvy and engaged, the data probably is better than if they are indifferent and bored. What the prediction software can't do is tell which of these input conditions prevails. Even for those groups that are engaged and savvy, the data processed first by the human mind, in all its analytical and intuitive abilities, gives a prediction edge only a few points higher than other methods and is not as reliable as some executives would like. What no one seems to be considering is how effective predictive market exercises are in helping maintain focus on the coherent story, not just trying to predict the future.

Regardless of prediction accuracy, getting an organization to believe in and act upon a coherent story that includes the future and its probabilities is the key. There were plenty of pundits predicting the turn-of-the-millennium dot-com burst, but not too many of them actually believed it. We believe that part of the answer to this phenomenon lies in the fact that more voices were claiming a continued path to the future based upon what had happened in the near term than conveying a story that covered a longer past-present-future time frame. Knowing the exact future doesn't confer the ability to navigate to it. Whether your story is pinned to the hopes of the tipping point, the long tail, or the J curve, it will be shaped by story belief and adaptation to changing realities.

Organizational Longevity

Is THE purpose of all companies to live and thrive indefinitely? Many, of course, argue that such longevity is highly desirable. A company that outlives your duration of employment not only confirms a job well done (it continues to exist), but it also appeals to the same part of our human nature that having children and grandchildren appeals to. We all want to feel that our lives matter and that somehow our time upon this planet will be remembered.

Corporate longevity also has practical consequences. If you are a stockholder or anticipate receiving some retirement benefits, then a solvent company is the guarantor. In some cultures having children is a familial version of this situation. But must all companies live forever?

Some argue that organizations exist for different reasons than for the people who populate them, and that survival-of-the-fittest dynamics will deal with the situation appropriately. Those who work in the companies that are attacked and subdued by predators or plague must simply understand that this is the nature of things.

Others, like Arie de Geus, argue that "Like all organisms, the living company exists primarily for its own survival and improvement: to fulfill its potential and to become as great as it can be."[31] One could take this statement and assume de Geus believes that companies should live indefinitely. In fact, his argument is very much the opposite. Using a type of anthropological analogy, he argues that a living company is different from an economic company. The goal of the economic company is to maximize opportunity, while the goal of the living company is to live up to its potential as it considers its political, social, and existential dynamics. In a way de Geus suggests that, like individuals, a living company's goal is to self-actualize. What matters is not immortality, but living up to the fullest extent of possibilities granted during the course of existence.

Regardless of viewpoint, the leader-as-navigator should take into account which view underlies the sentiment of the organization, for it will have a striking bearing on how to gain alignment and how to cope with adaptation.

4 *Architecture*

A HUNDRED and fifty years ago, coal tar was a waste product that was dumped into rivers or sluiced into vast pits dug for storage. Neither solution was particularly efficient, pleasant to the nose, nor environmentally friendly—and still isn't in those areas where coal tar waste is mismanaged. But the history of coal tar changed as the innovative chemists of the industrial revolution began to turn a waste product into an asset. Notable among these inventors was eighteen-year-old London chemical student William Perkin, who was among many across Europe attempting to synthesize quinine from the coal tar compound aniline, now used to make polyurethane. Working in his crude home laboratory in East London in 1856, one of Perkin's experiments yielded a dark violet substance that he was able to isolate and refine as a beautiful violet dye. He dubbed it *mauveine*, the first artificial aniline dye. Silk dyers in Lyon went crazy for the new color of dye, and by 1862 Queen Victoria was seen fashionably dressed in a new mauveine-dyed silk gown at the Royal Exhibition.[1]

Invention is crucial to business, but it requires business initiative to turn a good idea into a business proposition, and a sense of business architecture to create an organization that can sustain that business proposition. The discovery of coal tar dyes collided with an energetic entrepreneur, Friedrich Englehorn, who owned a coal gas operation in Mannheim, Germany. In the tradition of great business founders, Englehorn wanted to turn invention into an entire business process that spanned acquiring raw materials, processing them, producing final products, and establishing business channels for sale. In 1865 he founded Badische Anilin- und Soda-Fabrik, now known as BASF. What started out as a small factory in a small town has grown and innovated its way to become a world-recognized leader in the chemical, oil and gas, performance chemical, plastics, and agricultural products sectors. In a June 23, 2003, speech vice rector Karlheinz Meier of the University of Heidelberg compared the success story of BASF to "a 'chemical compound' made up of three components: scientific instinct, commercial acumen, and the courage to support change."[2] The rector thus recited three important components for the leader-as-architect. Many an authentic, energetic leader voicing a compelling vision has failed when he or she lacked the architectural skills to develop an organization that could implement the vision.

Today's business leaders need to create environments in which high-performance work systems can exist and develop, whether those systems are devoted to customer service, financial transactions, quality management, supplier interactions, or any of a host of other business activities. But these systems live inside the overall organizational design, which can either encourage the creation and perfection of work systems or strangle them altogether. During the transactional era, leaders generally defaulted to a pragmatic, historic type of organizational design that was inherited from command-and-control military and governmental organizations. During the transformational era, new organizational designs were created and the science of organizational design gained momentum. In both periods, the dominant mind-set suggested that organizational design was expressly a job for senior leaders. But beginning in the late transformational era, and into the current transcultural era, organizational design experts altered their observation as business models and business structures changed. Current levels of dynamism involving organization structure, roles, and business models have led transcultural-era observers like Nadler and Tushman to conclude, "The truth is that continuous design, at one level or another, will become a fact of life, and the successful managers will be those who can understand it, embrace it, and explain it to others, and help make it happen."[3]

This shift in design, being both continuous and spread among all managers, may be the single greatest reason for the current cry for better execution. This emphasis, which has been demonstrated in a myriad of business periodicals and an avalanche of books on the subject, is in one respect predictable. During times of expansion and new markets (think China and India), the business race often depends upon good execution. The source labor behind this preoccupation is architecture. The leader-as-architect role may initially seem more managerial in nature, but we argue that at its essence it is a critical piece of leadership.

The individual level of leadership for architecture involves creating and sustaining environments in which *high-performance work systems* can be invented and maintained. At the organizational level the leader-as-architect must look at the overall *dynamic design* of the organization and ensure that the organizational structure supports the company's vision and strategy. As the environment changes and the leader-as-navigator adapts, then the leader-as-navigator must redesign the organization.

Failing to attend to the labor of architecture can have dire consequences. Old architectures in new economies rarely survive forever, even though they may take decades to recognize the signs of their own demise. Remaining architecturally relevant is the antidote to what Larry Bossidy and Ram Charan call "structurally defective industries": "Companies in these industries are chronically unable to earn enough to be economically successful, no matter how brilliant their strategies may be or how meticulously they execute. Their business models are broken and can't be fixed."[4]

Friedrich Englehorn was a business innovator in the early years of the industrial revolution, and one of his abilities was to apply a leader-as-architect eye toward the building of BASF. By thinking through the entire process of turning invention into commercial venture, he created organizational mechanisms that allowed BASF to grow and expand into the many markets it now serves. Over time, the company's attention to work processes that can create efficiency and innovation, as well as to the overall design concept, has led BASF to its *Verbund* concept. *Verbund* means "integrated, networked, or linked" to the maximum degree possible. As we will see later, this is an exciting organizational design example.

High-Performance Work Systems

INNOVATION is a word people both love and hate. We love it when it actually happens and we create the to-die-for new product or process that fills the coffers and strengthens the brand. We hate it when we spend money on it, spend more money on it, and wonder why invention and investment are strangers to each other. As Rosabeth Moss Kanter points out: "Innovation is back at the top of the corporate agenda. Never a fad, but always in or out of fashion, innovation gets rediscovered as a growth enabler every half-dozen years (about the length of a managerial generation). Too often, however, grand declarations about innovation are followed by mediocre execution that produces anemic results, and innovation groups are quietly disbanded in cost-cutting drives. Each generation embarks on the same enthusiastic quest for the next new thing and faces the same challenge of overcoming innovation stiflers."[5]

We often think innovation or invention is something to be pursued in and of itself, but in reality it is the predictable outcome of an organization's ability to pursue high-performance systems in a manner that allows creativity, excellence, invention, and perfection to coexist. How do individual leaders create environments in which high-performance work systems can endure? It's not simple, nor linear, nor for the fainthearted. Sloppy prototyping and constant improvement are part of the equation. Refinement of process and fine-tuning of procedure are also part of the equation. But leaders in their individual capacity must help their communities grapple with creating new processes, new inventions, new procedures, and new techniques as well. The tension between refining the known and discovering the unknown is at the heart of high-performance work systems and is the individual labor for the leader-as-architect. The following three contemporary expressions serve to illustrate how this is accomplished.

Creative Tension

IN HIS thoughtful book *The Creativity Priority*, Jerry Hirshberg sums up an idea he and his team used to their advantage during his tenure with Nissan Design International: "[I]t is the creative abrasion of tiny air molecules that creates the beauty of a shooting star, without which it would be just another rapidly moving, cold, anonymous piece of rock."[6] Hirshberg's team at Nissan collected an impressive array of design awards, both inside and outside the automotive industry. "Creative tension" is our version of his "creative abrasion."

The idea is to simply create a bit of friction and see what happens. Friction can be created when opposing viewpoints are vigorously discussed, competing processes are funded in parallel, people are placed together on project teams made up of individuals who are great at their craft but may not work so well together, or ambiguity is allowed to exist longer than rapid decision-making philosophy can tolerate. At the September 27, 2000, Crave Conference, held at the Yerba Buena Conference Center in San Francisco, Hirshberg told a story about his idea of "providing your staff and yourself opportunities for ambivalence—periods of not knowing which way is best."[7] He recounted how in the 1980s the American bias to be the first to market collided with the Japanese bias to be the best in the marketplace. The event he was referring to occurred in 1983 during Nissan's initial venture into designing a sport utility vehicle. Japanese managers at first found it odd that people would want a vehicle that would literally operate off the road. Not only would drivers of such vehicles violate transportation rules—or so it seemed to the Japanese at that time—but they would do so in vehicles that seemed "rough-hewn and impolite." They decided Americans were more suited to such ideas and gave the project to Hirshberg's team.

During a meeting to discuss production and scheduling, the debate tension between being first or best led to a poignant moment of silence. Hirshberg recounted that he interrupted the impasse by thanking his Japanese counterparts and adjourning the meeting. He wanted to allow the different cultural viewpoints to permeate both sides' worldviews. This took more than two months of pondering and reflection. The end result was not just an increased tolerance of each other's point of view (diversity), but also an alteration in thinking (innovation) from both cultures. Comparing this experience to his tenure at General Motors, Hirshberg said this ambivalence produced a breakthrough that resulted in "a vehicle that was closer to the designer's original conceptual sketch than anything I'd ever done in Detroit, where there was no culture, or language, or geographic barrier."

Maintaining a bias toward creative tension is difficult, because creating more efficient processes often means turning to the refinement of old ideas rather than the creation of new ones. But once a leader develops an environment in which creative tension can become a process in and of itself, any refinement process, such as Six

Sigma, can be adopted as a resource for creative tension. The Six Sigma process advocates both new idea generation and idea refinement. As Annemieke van der Werff and Tamra Tammen suggest, "Once Six Sigma language is adopted by the organization, it begins to focus on productive activities instead of conversation about productive activities."[8] Creative tension can become ingrained behavior.

Rampant Virtuosity

INTERVIEWING for a new job is often an open, robust process that employers use to gain a broad range of feeling about a person's capability, experiences, and education. Yet once the person is hired, the procedures and processes of the organization, along with individual managers' biases and rush to execution, seem to erode and narrow the new employee's broad talent down to a few specific skills. Over the past twenty years, in Western culture we have increased our ability to detect and evaluate genius, but we still struggle with how to put it to work.

Gordon MacKenzie recounts this process of socialization and standardization in the opening chapter of his insightful and delightful book *Orbiting the Giant Hairball*. He used to represent Hallmark Cards at local Kansas City school districts, and to illustrate the concept of creativity he would show the children how a sculpture artist worked. For several years he conducted about a dozen yearly visits to schools, and during these daylong visits each grade from first to last would retire to the gymnasium, where this gifted man would not simply entertain them, but would conjure a special magic over their minds.

MacKenzie asked the same question to each group and every time would receive the same disturbing yet predictable answer. The question was "How many of you are an artist?" First graders all leaped from their seats and waved their arms. This level of exuberance fell to 50 percent for second graders, and by the third grade it dropped to roughly a third. By the time the sixth graders arrived and filed obediently onto the gym floor, only one or two kids were willing or able to identify themselves as artists. MacKenzie's conclusion was that the nature of socialization, while a necessary process, suppresses the development of creative genius.[9]

Business socialization suppresses creativity, too, but at a more rapid pace. We hire the gifted and then give them a rulebook that effectively stifles the range of their creative thought. We insist they develop business skills to the suppression of other natural talents. We don't mean it, we don't want it, but unfortunately we do it. We do it so well, in fact, that we have to institute training either during college or during employment to counteract the basic normalization process that all societies employ to help create functioning human interactions.

"It's not cool people that create cool projects. Cool projects bring out individuals' genius," Michael Schrage once declared in an interview with Julie Anixter, who at the time was with Tom Peters Company.[10] We agree with the fundamental premise his statement prompts one to consider: really cool projects stimulate individuals to use their various talents, whether they are business skills or not. Managers who understand this actually create conditions in which a person's virtuosity is allowed full range of expression. To us, the idea of virtuosity springs from the roots of the words *virtuosity* and *virtuoso*, terms that involve virtues, talents, abilities, and developed skills—those native or acquired abilities that need not be compartmentalized just because you are "at work." And there's nothing like an interesting project to stimulate creative tension, to engage the entire range of a person's abilities.

Continuous Play

GORDON MACKENZIE was with Hallmark Cards for thirty years, and those colleagues of ours who saw him deliver public presentations said he was the most original, most engaging speaker they had ever heard—and some of our colleagues are highly paid, terrific speakers in their own right. In our telephone conversations with Gordon, we did get a sense of his personal humor, warmth, and genius, but unfortunately he passed away before we could meet him in person. One of his last jobs at Hallmark was an unusual posting that allowed him to select his own managerial title—"Creative Paradox." He decorated his office in a style reminiscent of Merlin and magic. And according to what he confessed in his book, the most significant thing he did during his three years in this role was to say, "Yes, I think it could work," to the variety of people who brought him ideas.[11]

Gordon's point of view is that organizations often generate an epidemic of "no," and that "yes" is the only antidote. Expanding his keen observation further, we assert that if you want adults to engage in the serious business of continuous play—that is, the ability to continually come up with wacky ideas in the pursuit of those that can work—then turn the tide from "no" to "yes."

INSEAD, the world-renowned graduate business school in Fontainebleau, France, is devoting time and attention to helping managers and MBA students learn how to manage creativity, not just process and finance. The school has teamed with the Art Center College of Design in Pasadena, California, to create a fourteen-week course that helps participants learn not just lateral thinking and blue-sky conceptualizing, but also how to manage the messy and nonlinear process of innovation and design. The students in this course are learning to engage in continuous play. Some of the development projects that teams are presented with are a high-end luggage suite for female business travelers with special compartments and wheels that make it easier to pull, running shoes that indicate when the shock absorbers are wearing down, and a professional lunch box that would appeal to high-end grocers or Weight Watchers.

"Working with design students has opened our minds," said Christine Hutcheson, a thirty-four-year-old INSEAD participant. Her team worked on the lunch box problem and developed a solution they called the Contigo. In an interview about her experience, she said, "If you had just put five MBAs in a room with this project, they would have taken a three-ring binder, put it in a Ziploc bag, and punched holes in it," she says.[12]

Tom Kelley, general manager of IDEO, suggests the following in his book *The Art of Innovation:* "Prototyping, brainstorming, and observations. These are the fundamentals, the reading, writing, and arithmetic of innovation. Great teams provide the charge that makes these basic skills flow throughout the company."[13] We would suggest that such skills are essential for creating a work environment that fosters continuous play.

Dynamic Design

"WE CANNOT return to a simpler world. Much of contemporary social criticism is made irrelevant by its refusal to face that fact...We must live in the modern world. We cannot stem the pressure for more intricate organization of our economy, our production, our social, political, and cultural life. We must master the new forms of organization or they will master us."[14] John W. Gardner wrote this in 1964 during the height of the transactional period of leadership, when the eruptive cauldron of social change that would lead us to the transformational era of leadership was still simmering below the surface. As a deep thinker, Gardner was pointing to the future, trying in his way to loosen transactional period command-and-control styles of thinking. His thoughts are echoed in the thinking and research of contemporary writers and researchers who have studied change and organizational design.

Whether you subscribe to a systems view or an organism view as your guiding analogy to organizations, nearly all researchers have concluded that organizations change and adapt as a direct result of contending with three powerful forces: history, strategy, and environment. In order to create functioning systems and processes that match the intentions of organization leaders, their strategies must work in the context of the business environment. Adaptation should occur at least at the same rate at which the environment is changing. So strategy forms from environmental cues that motivate leaders to overcome the inertia of an organization's history. Basically, organizational leaders must attend to system-wide issues, both internal and external. And as Gardner pointed out, there is no return to simpler times. The three contemporary expressions of these issues for the organizational leader-as-architect are detailed next.

Matchless Business Model

MICHAEL PORTER'S influence upon business thinking is well known and noted. Not only has he stimulated the business community to think in macroeconomic terms, but over the past twenty years he has also supplied several ideas that have inspired leaders to consider organizational dynamics in a fundamentally different manner. Among

Porter's ideas are the three generic strategies of cost leadership, differentiation, and focus. As the world has adapted to these ideas, among others, many companies have become better at positioning their organizations in the larger economic marketplace, or ecology.

Considering that these three generic approaches define how organizations create value propositions, inevitable sardine packing results. There are only three strategies and a vast number of companies. Each organization pursuing any one of these strategies must consider doing it better than their numerous competitors. By following a matchless business model, a company's strategy can help it to retain a long-term competitive edge regardless of whether it uses a low-cost, differentiation, or focus strategy.

For example, Microsoft's famous operating system deal with IBM was a focus strategy. It allowed Microsoft such an early edge, with such a long-term commitment, which essentially prevented other entrants into the market, that the arrangement produced a matchless business model. Even today, operating systems are by far the largest contributor to Microsoft's profits. In its 2006 annual report, Microsoft reported that platforms (Windows XP, Windows Media, and other operating systems) brought in $13 billion of the company's $44 billion in total revenue, but supplied $10 billion of the $16 billion in profits.[15] This has been a matchless business model since Microsoft's inception.

Seamless Structure

LUDWIGSHAFEN is a small city on the Rhine River that was originally a fort built to protect the city on the other side, Mannheim. Notables born in Ludwigshafen include philosopher Ernst Bloch and former German chancellor Helmut Kohl, but the city's commercial history is tied to the growth of BASF. In 1865 BASF moved some of its facilities from Mannheim to the Ludwigshafen area, and today the city hosts BASF's headquarters.

Jürgen Hambrecht, the chief executive of BASF, describes the BASF site as "ultimate business cluster," which is fitting for the world's largest integrated (*Verbund*) chemical site.[16] More than one thousand miles of piping, one hundred miles of rail, several hundred intermodal transport terminals, and a logistics terminal that holds a hefty one million pallets are all contained within a four-square-mile campus that employs more than thirty-six thousand workers. If a worker doesn't want to ride the rail, he or she can simply walk or jump on one of the company's many red bicycles to move from one facility to another. This cluster-style plant works because of an emphasis on efficiencies and a devotion to work systems that simply coax every extra erg of value from every chemical or chemical reaction. Analysis suggests that in energy and infrastructure costs alone, this cluster style saves BASF more than $256 million (€200 million) per year over managing the same number of facilities that are operating separately and often at some distance from one another. While other companies worry about remaining sensitive to rapidly changing markets, BASF focuses its overall organizational design to integration and systems. Its *Verbund* strategy has been successful, and BASF has deployed this same concept in China, Malaysia, Belgium, and the United States.

For example, integrating supplier relations has been an ongoing process since the early days of the TQM (total quality management) revolution. BASF's approach is to help coordinate and link international operations with its expertise so that local managers can make more informed choices. Thomas Lanzerath, who is responsible for plant equipment procurement, must look for global players who can work with BASF from Kunsan, South Korea, to Concon, Chile, to Mangalore, India, to Morganton, North Carolina. Lanzerath's network systems are so well tuned that he can help local managers make better decisions. For him it's a process that is not command-and-control central purchasing, but "decentralized coordination" that works "because everyone is so committed to the success of the idea."[17] This commitment to the design idea of *Verbund* results in continuous improvements to the work systems throughout BASF that allow it to achieve optimum and advantageous workflow.

BASF offers a study in dynamic design. In a world where many chemical companies are experimenting with smaller, more numerous, and physically separated sites, BASF is continuing to design and improve the cluster concept. But it is not just replicating the system because it has evolved well over the years. The management team at BASF is constantly exploring the environment and testing for ways they can maintain efficiency in a dynamically changing world. Current efforts are focused on bringing a type of virtual *Verbund* to the marketplace. Instead of one company in the cluster, several share the same campus. This concept brings cluster-style efficiencies to many different chemical companies that can take advantage of the physically adjacent efficiencies and still remain separate operating entities.

Flawless Mission-Critical Systems

"'WE'RE very comfortable being misunderstood,' Jeff Bezos says, letting loose one of his famously thunderous laughs. 'We've had lots of practice.'"[18] Amazon.com is a household name in most countries around the world, and the company has ridden a twelve-year roller coaster of success, near misses, close calls, and rebounds that seem to stalk online retail systems. This most influential online innovator has endured many years of nonprofitability, which has prompted many analysts to declare its demise, even referring to it as "Amazon.toast" back in 1997 when Barnes & Noble launched their online operation. At this moment in 2007, that earlier prediction seems not just premature, but uninformed as well. Amazon initially reacted to the Barnes & Noble move as competition, but quickly realized that this view was both a losing strategy and the wrong one for Internet growth.

So Bezos shifted focus. "What we want to do is become the Earth's most customer-centric company. By doing so, we want other companies to copy us. If we get other companies to do that, that's something I'll be very proud of."[19] In large measure, Amazon has indeed been a trailblazer, inspiring many to follow the company's lead. And a significant part of that lead has to do with Amazon's impeccable and easy-to-use systems. According to the *BusinessWeek* cover story about Bezos and Amazon in its November 13, 2006, issue: "Amazon has spent 12 years and $2 billion perfecting many of the pieces behind its online store. By most accounts, those operations are now among the biggest and most reliable in the world."[20]

And now it seems Amazon wants to offer these highly effective systems to others. It wants to rent out rack space in its ten million square feet of warehouses worldwide, as well as its spare computing capacity, data storage, and some of the software code it has written that enables Amazon to run its business. In essence, Amazon wants to become an online digital utility. This is a big gamble, and many analysts have deep doubts about its eventual success. Time will tell the tale, but at first glance the idea is tempting. Who wouldn't want to take advantage of using highly reliable—perhaps even flawless—online systems proven by thousands of customers each day from Amazon?

The basic idea behind flawless systems is that every business has a certain few systems that must work all the time, everywhere. The savvy, trusted organization can identify these systems and invests heavily to ensure the best processes are used.

Counterpoint to Architecture

WORDS like *work systems, business models, structure, roles and responsibilities,* and *procedures* are all associated with management tasks. In the transactional age one of the most familiar exercises that leaders and students of leadership debated was the difference between leadership and management. And although the debates raged over particulars, the themes were highly similar. Leadership tends to focus on people and interpersonal issues; issues such as credibility, motivation, inspiration, and engagement stem from this mental model. Management, on the other hand, tends to focus on things; issues such as monitoring, scheduling, task completion, counting, and measuring flow from this point of view. Interestingly, encouragement is often divided between the two. The interpersonal pat on the back is more often associated with leadership, while "bonus" is more often associated with managerial reward systems. This exercise tends to create a useful dichotomy for individual leadership (inspiration versus expense tracking), but it usually leads to unresolved debates when it comes to organizational leadership (designing a business model versus executing against it).

For example, challenging conventional views, creativity, innovation, and all the other terms that have to do with seeing something new tend to be more associated with leadership. Continuous improvement, with its emphasis on metrics and analysis, quality control, supply chain transactions, and all other terms that involve controlling things (even new things) seems to be more associated with management. This is why architecture seems often to be more managerial oriented than leadership oriented. But as we have shown, the leadership aspects of architecture have to do with developing an environment where innovation can take place (individual leader-as-architect) and having a mindfulness of dynamic design in terms of the organization (organizational leader-as-architect).

Some critics would counter these distinctions as mere semantics, asserting that most, if not all, of the aspects of leader-as-architect are more grounded in the hands-on nature of getting things done. Others limit their view of leader-as-architect and associate it with either developing a solid, wealth-producing business model or with making sure that systems and structure allow for the fullest implementation of the strategy. Both of these views seem to have more of a business-management nature. If you support either of these views, then it may seem more difficult to see much leadership in the labor of architecture.

5 Community

THE LONG-ADMIRED and well-known Aspen Institute states that its mission is "to foster enlightened leadership and open-minded dialogue."[1] We applaud this ambitious goal and the vigor with which the institution encourages leaders to reflect deeply upon big issues. In the mid-1990s the Aspen Institute decided, along with many other organizations, to devote some of its time and energy to next-generation leadership development. This sparked then–executive vice president James O'Toole to write a book reflecting upon values-based leadership and how the premise of values could unite individuals in a common cause. While the book was ostensibly about change, O'Toole stimulated us to consider that change is simply noise until it becomes communal and focused.[2] Sometimes the source of community focus is a person, sometimes it's a disruptive event, and sometimes such focus stems from a powerful idea. But what happens after the change?

In his book *Leading Change: The Argument for Values-Based Leadership*, O'Toole uses an unusual device to get people to consider the nature of leadership and community in times of change. He asks his readers to consider James Ensor's painting *Christ Entering Brussels in 1889* as a reflection tool that stimulates a discussion about creating followership in modernity.[3] Ensor was a Belgian expressionist painter who lived from 1860 to 1949. His paintings are displayed in many famous museums in North America, Belgium, France, Spain, and Australia.[4] O'Toole interprets the imagery of this particular painting in terms of leadership: "Ensor causes us to wonder how anyone could lead from the middle of an inattentive crowd of individualists, each a political and social equal, and every last one bent on demonstrating that fact."[5]

O'Toole's premise has to do with change and how leaders can effect it in modern times, when not only is individualism at an all-time high, but when the idea of workers as free agents has gained considerable attention as well. He asks three questions at the beginning of his book: "Can change be commanded?" "Can leaders achieve change by manipulating followers?" "Can change be shepherded?"[6] The answers to these questions are complex, but O'Toole builds a credible case for using a values-based (what we have termed "authenticity") approach coupled with an inspiring vision that is built on followers' aspirations (what we have termed "navigation").

Being inspired by O'Toole's use of imagery, we commissioned a fabulously talented Vancouver, British Columbia, artist, Naomi Topuzoglu, to construct a painting for us, but with contemporary imagery of a nonreligious nature. Our painting, titled *The Procession*, is reproduced on the facing page.

We use *The Procession* as a point of focus and inspiration in asking the following questions:

+ *In what ways does this image remind you of your organization?*

+ *What leadership questions does this image stimulate you to consider?*

+ *Where are you in the image? How many different parts of your identity are reflected in different parts of this image?*

+ *How would you go about building community if all the people in this image worked for your organization?*

Our intent in asking these kinds of questions is not to guide a discussion about change, but to guide a discussion about leadership in general and community in particular. For while many organizations have authentic leaders, values-based organizational guidance, and inspiring visions, there is still widespread workforce dissatisfaction that moves many contemporary authors and theorists to discuss the lack of genuine community in modern organizations. John W. Gardner suggested that leadership failure could nearly always be traced to a breakdown in a sense of community. His experience led him to conclude, "Leaders are community builders because they have to be."[7]

We believe that authentic leaders who have helped create an inspiring mission or cause and have built a sound system for imple-

menting work against this cause still have the slippery underlyingla-
bor of community with which they must grapple. At the individual
level of leadership this labor of leader-as-community-builder concerns *engagement*. Helping associates and professionals maintain a
devotion to career, task, and vision has a daily, individual component.
For the organizational leader-as-community-builder, the central task
is *perpetual leadership*. This entails the constant development of
leadership abilities throughout the organization that not only complements engagement matters but also assures a steady supply of
leadership over time.

Marcus Buckingham and Curt Coffman of the Gallup Management Organization are recognized for promoting greater understanding of the ideas of engagement, disengagement, and active disengagement.[8] Donald Kantor and Philip Mirvis's book, *The Cynical Americans*, anticipated Gallup's data set by a decade.[9] The issues of motivation, engagement, worker satisfaction, building the most-admired company, and creating the most-inspired workplace are common expressions that concern the central leadership labor of building and maintaining a committed community.

Engagement

MANFRED KETS DE VRIES is an experienced consultant and therapist who has interacted with a great many highly placed organizational leaders. He has dealt with leaders who use fear to stimulate engagement, and has found that while at times this can produce results, it always produces toxic political climates. Forced engagement seems oxymoronic, yet many of us are tempted to use forceful means under certain conditions. Kets de Vries cites a case in which he asked senior executives to use a one-to-ten scale to rate their work experience in terms of how much fun they had in their jobs, and the ratings were all below four. He repeated the exercise a week later when the CEO and a group of senior executives were present, and the ratings were in the eight-to-ten range. He was amazed at the rapid organizational transformation. In organizations such as these, he believes, "candor flees authority."[10]

Nearly everyone in the research community suggests that the longer-term, and better, path to productivity and engagement is to resist the urge to use fear. These theorists and practitioners have applied their insights to systems that can promote engagement. Such systems run the gamut from intrinsic/extrinsic motivation theory, to the psychology of needs, to appreciative inquiry, to compensation theory, to outsourcing strategies. While each of these systems approach individual and community productivity and motivation from a different angle, all are attempting to get to the basics of engagement.

Our view of engagement consists of a three-part system. For true long-term engagement to exist, people must be genuinely appre-

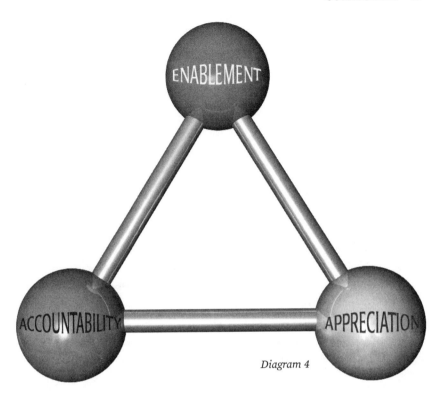

Diagram 4

ciated, enabled to do their specific work, and held accountable for their contributions not only by themselves but also by the organization. We have organized these ideas in the following model (Diagram 4), which deliberately looks like it might come from a chemistry or biochemistry textbook. We have done this to show that while each "atom" of this molecule can exist independently, in order to create what we call the "engagement molecule" all three atoms must to be bound together.

A simple way to understand this triune system is to conduct the following thought experiment. Cover up one of the three parts of the engagement molecule, or model, and as you look at the remaining two, ask yourself the following question: "What kind of organization would I have if I had just these two components of the model?" Consider the nature of the work, the kind of climate you'd expect, and how associates in the system might feel. We encourage you to try this idea as you read this part of our book.

Contemporary Outcomes for Individual Community

WE WILL explore possible answers to this thought problem as we examine each of the components in turn. In his rant on leadership, Tom Peters proclaims a golden leadership triangle comprised of "(1) *Talent Fanatic-Mentor*... (2) *Creator Visionary*... (3) *Inspired Profit Mechanic*." A full third of his sixty ideas on leadership concern one of the three parts of our engagement molecule, including the following statement: "Great Leaders on Snorting Steeds Are Important—but <u>Great Talent Developers</u> *(Type I Leadership)* are the Bedrock of Organizations that Perform Over the Long Haul."[11] Max DePree, in his elegant book *Leadership Is an Art*, suggests in a section on the rights of work, "Each of us, no matter what our rank in the hierarchy may be, has the same rights: to be needed, to be involved, to have a covenantal relationship, to understand the corporation, to affect our destiny, to be accountable, to appeal, to make a commitment."[12] His reflections seem to suggest that rather than a condition to be adjusted by management, engagement is a right of working itself. Instead of community, DePree uses the powerful and unusual term *covenantal*—meaning that which binds us firmly together—to express the intensity of his conviction about these rights of engagement.

A good example of binding community and what it means to have a covenantal relationship can be found in the experiences of the U.S. Army during World War II. Rich Anderson recounts how policy was altered through the direct experience of the power of community in an article on replacing troops.

> Once a soldier was separated from his unit by wounds or illness, there was little chance of him returning to that unit. Instead, he was sent to a replacement depot, a repple-depple in Army slang. From the depot he would then be reassigned as needed to whatever unit had a shortfall in his particular MOS (military occupation specialty). This meant that a soldier could spend months of training, forming close bonds with comrades, the basis for unit cohesion, and then in his first day of combat could be separated from them, never to fight with them again. This system of individual replacement caused many soldiers to disguise illness and wounds so they could stay with their units. Other soldiers, in hospital, went AWOL (absent-without-leave) so as to rejoin their units. It wasn't until 1945 that the individual replacement system

was modified to allow a majority of sick and wounded soldiers to rejoin their unit after recovering.[13]

Genuinely Appreciated

WHEN you covered up the appreciation component of the engagement model, did you envision, as we did, an organization that could seem mechanical, even lifeless? Work gets done with enablement and accountability, but can it be sustained or even enjoyed without some measure of appreciation? Many people we have asked to complete this exercise suggest that the organizational model that results from removing the appreciation element is similar to a sweatshop. So what does appreciation add that completes the engagement cycle?

In order to answer this question, we need to deal with what appreciation is and what it is not. Appreciation stems from a deeper mind-set, a way of seeing others that is deeper and richer than merely maintaining a positive attitude about people. Having a positive attitude toward others is helpful, but it is limited in that it tends to narrow one's focus to simple constructs such as looking at the good with the bad, finding a silver lining in any action or situation, or maintaining the hope that things will get better. All of these mental qualities are helpful, but an appreciative mind-set goes even further.

Basic defining terms for appreciation from the dictionary include "sensitive awareness, recognition of an aesthetic value, expressing admiration or gratitude." In other words, appreciation isn't just observing exterior actions, but it's also considering deeper levels of personal aesthetics, values, or potentials and then expressing admiration or gratitude for these qualities *even in the absence of any particular external behavior.* We argue that appreciation is a way of seeing the entire potential of another person and constructing a vibrant, unique, and ongoing image of who and what that person is becoming. This implies, of course, that the leader gets to know the person's talent well enough so that the image construction can become as specific as possible. Then all appreciative comments can be constructed as a reminder to the person that he is constantly in the process of becoming his future self, or the best portion of who he truly is. This appeal nearly always stimulates positive feelings, improved work attitudes, and a desire for performance enhancement. It takes nourishment to the person's roots, rather than just applying reinforcement to particular surface-level actions.

An appreciative mind-set goes further than just nourishing the individual. It also affects the system. By maintaining an appreciative mind-set, the individual leader significantly moderates a variety of leader-member exchanges that can have unintended consequences. Although a great many studies have shown that people respond well to task-contingent rewards, especially when tasks are clear and the reward structure is fairly applied, there are limits to these transactional systems. In a comprehensive review of the major theories, Bernard Bass concluded: "As an approach to effective leadership, contingent reinforcement has considerable limitations, although it may work well in many situations. Rewards for performance and disciplinary actions for failures may not work as expected for numerous reasons, ranging from the leader's lack of control over what the followers are seeking to the overriding impact of group norms. In the last analysis, the carrot-and-stick approach may make the subordinate feel denigrated and less than an adult person."[14]

There are certainly known methods of administering rewards and recognition that do have positive results, and they have been incorporated into our model of engagement.[15] But the key ingredient is the appreciative mind-set. Seeing others as whole human beings, with potential beyond what they currently demonstrate, and a capacity for growth that may or may not have evidence to support it, has powerful effects both on the leader and his or her followers. When an appreciative mind-set is adopted by leaders at the individual level, it not only allows contingent rewards to be distributed within context and sufficient meaning applied to these rewards, but it also allows the leader to add confirming messages to the person regarding his higher potential. An appreciative mind-set is essential to helping the person see that he is not just being rewarded for task accomplishment, but that he is also being recognized for the person he is becoming.

Steven Berglas suggests this happens even to top-notch players. He described a scenario about a high-performing Harvard graduate as follows: "Jane's problem was that she felt underappreciated. She consistently overperformed, and her boss said she did great work. This was the highest accolade he ever gave anyone, but Jane needed more. She worked harder and harder, but more fulsome praise never came her way."[16] Berglas goes on to describe more "A" players' difficulties, but his example strikes at the heart of the issue. This "A" player was already doing such great work that her leader's response was predictable: She was rewarded with money, advancement, and praise for her work (fundamental rewards for "contingent performance"). But she was not recognized for who she was or for the personal qualities she brought to the situation, and the boss likely failed to create an image of her potential future abilities, because her performance was already at such high levels.

Even when they receive extrinsic rewards such as bonuses for specific work achievements, people may feel personally slighted, or that the achievement is tainted, when one of the following all-too-familiar things happens during the distribution of the reward:

- *The person's name is mispronounced or misspelled.*

- *The person delivering the reward is uncertain about the specifics of the situation and fumbles when relating the the story about why the person is being rewarded.*

- *The leader distributing the reward is mistrusted.*

- *The leader distributing the reward does not appear genuine in his or her manner.*

- *The reward announcement is accompanied by additional remarks that are not pertinent to the occasion or in some manner defame or denigrate the person receiving the reward.*

Specifically Enabled

REMOVE the idea of enablement—that condition in which developed expertise meshes gears with opportunity and resources—and what is the resulting organization? Many have said it's like living in third-world poverty. The culture may be appreciative and individuals held accountable for the actions they engage in, but there's not much for them to work on. Long-term scarce resources or insufficiently trained workers create an impoverished condition.

Muhammad Yunus and Grameen Bank received the 2006 Nobel Peace Prize in recognition of their thirty years of efforts to create economic and social development through a system of "microcredit." Yunus has proven that enabling the poor can release pent-up ability, ignite engagement, and change society. When Adam Smith, editor in chief of the Nobel Prize organization, called Yunus to inform him that he was to receive the prize, Smith asked if there was any particular message Yunus wanted to give to the public. Yunus said: "The one message that we are trying to promote all the time, that poverty in the world is an artificial creation. It doesn't belong to human civilization, and we can change that, we can make people come out of poverty and have the real state of affairs."[17]

Following Yunus's profound mode of thinking, we suggest that enabled or disabled workers are the result of what leaders and followers artificially create. The sources of enablement or empowerment are well known, and the application of these sources to increase a person's ability to work seems an obvious tool. But more than just general skills, the person must become specifically enabled to conduct specific work, and the problem with this often does not lie with that person's abilities, but with artificially created leadership restraints.

Information, authority, budget, clear time frames, access to others, and support are among the most commonly cited components of enablement cited by people as being necessary to create a truly engaged workplace. Leaders say that when this engaged workplace is in place, they gain the gifts of more time for organizational leadership issues, increased satisfaction, increased performance in their unit, greater visibility to upper management, and an increased willingness to represent their constituents.

So what gets in the way of these desirable outcomes? The answer for both leaders and talent is straightforward. Sharing information, authority, and access requires leaders to cede control, and that is among the most difficult tasks for leaders. On the talent side, making decisions, committing to time frames, being accountable for resource use, and sharing information requires initiative and courage, qualities that are often difficult for people to demonstrate. It is often easier, less painful, and less politically contentious to take the low, safe road.

These same conditions come into play when very specific skill sets are required. For example, technology alone has forced talented people everywhere to learn to cope with skills that were never learned during formal schooling, and technology enhancements do not appear to be slowing down. So when new technology becomes a requirement for people to complete their jobs, leaders must provide time and resources for them to learn the skills (and learn it themselves), and those people must in turn apply their ability to learn the skills or face the consequences of lowering their value to the organization.

Appropriately Accountable

THE THIRD part of the engagement model concerns accountability. When we have asked people to cover this element of the model and consider the resulting organizational type, the answers we often get include governmental agencies, civil service groups, or university organizations. While this is an unfair and inaccurate assessment (many fine examples of highly effective agencies, civil service groups, and universities can be cited), there are enough bad examples for most of us to understand why these come to mind as places where accountability is in short supply.

The truth is, however, that all organizations grapple with accountability issues. Some of our current clients are well-known companies with very recognizable brand names, and yet they are struggling with accountability issues because they have large, dominating percentages of the marketplace. Other clients are under the influence of merger issues. Some are facing accountability issues resulting from growth expectations. In each case, organizational leaders are focusing attention on individual accountability due to appropriate pressure, but the pushback universally concerns the appropriateness of the accountability.

In the case of the dominant market share situations, accountability issues are tied either to the scale of the operation or to market saturation. The major questions raised in such cases surround creating a culture of accountability when most actions, even by relatively high-level managers, rarely account for the full result. These leaders struggle with the sheer number of network connections arising from any decision or task over which they have no control. To be held accountable for an entire outcome when they have control of less than half seems so unfair that politicking becomes the smokescreen of choice for distancing oneself from accountability. Merger situations are fraught with concerns about redundancy, authority, influence, and other issues, and the sheer amount of conflicting information during the early stages dissuades leaders from committing to outcomes. In growth situations it would seem that accountability might be established more easily, but leaders are often overwhelmed by the scale of the task output required to attain the growth. Alternately, in cases where a company is trying to grow in a low- or no-growth marketplace, signing up for outcomes that may simply not be achievable feels inappropriate.

Regardless of the context, it is appropriateness that counts in accountability, for as all three of these typical situations indicate, accountability shares its role with enablement and appreciation. Telling people that they are accountable for a task without sufficient levels of authority or resources is a recipe for disappointment. Their response will generally fall between two extremes. They will try to increase their ability to get the task done either by assuming more authority than is granted or by siphoning resources, even illegally in the most drastic cases, in order to match their enablement levels with their accountability levels. Or they will allow their frustration to erode their motivation, retreat from doing their best, and in the worst cases simply resign themselves to their lack of ability. If they resort to this extreme, they may simply find ways to embed themselves in the system, protect their jobs, and live with lackluster performance, believing they are justified in their attitude. Or they will exit the company, and leaders are then left with trying to find those who will work in an untenable situation.

And even when accountability and enablement are balanced, it is appreciation that uses up the majority of the extra effort (often referred to as "discretionary" as if some of a person's effort is not under his or her discretion). The appreciative mind-set is the part of the engagement model that amps up enablement and accountability to higher-than-contracted levels.

Perpetual Leadership

BREAN MURRAY Institutional Research reported in 2004 that the growth of information technology in India would increase fivefold by 2008, for a total of $50 billion.[18] And a study from Gartner Research suggests in 2006 that global spending in IT will increase from its 2004 level of $193 billion to $260 billion by 2009, much of that slotted for India.[19] The Bangalore campus of Infosys Technologies is architecturally gorgeous, with the usual allotment of software campus amenities—recreational facilities, multiple restaurants, sculpted grounds, and, of course, yoga studios (this is India, after all). Thomas Friedman suggests that he began his journey to the conclusion that the world is flat (also the title of his highly acclaimed book) while standing in the Nandan Nikelani conference room situated on the Infosys campus.[20] A landslide of research has thundered into our consciousness and decision making about outsourcing jobs to India and other regions of the world where talent grows.

Yet in the hallways and public areas of GE Capital's offices all over India, signs are posted declaring, "Trespassers will be recruited."[21] The reason? There is an insufficient supply of talent in India for the number of software and technical jobs available there. Wage inflation and turnover, both of which are predictable in booming economies, also stifle organizations' ability to attract and retain talent. India's NASSCOM (National Association of Software and Service Companies) cites research that uses warfare metaphors to describe the broader picture of what is going on: "The four biggies [Microsoft, IBM, Oracle, SAP] are currently engaged in a fierce battle for the mindshare and client base in the next theatres of war... And to succeed, they are vying to create the most inclusive and comprehensive ecosystems. Further, to get there, they need large armies of partners to deliver the last mile solutions, and ought to give these ecosystems the tools to succeed and retain their loyalties." NASSCOM predicts that by 2010 there will be five hundred thousand fewer professionals available than needed in India.[22]

The economies of India and China are growing at such a rapid rate that country-grown companies there are outsourcing jobs to other countries such as the Philippines and Viet Nam. Just as Asia has become the answer to North America's and Europe's thirst for talent, so has the farther East become the answer to India's thirst for talent.

Add to this talent situation the predictions from pundits such as Robert Morison, Tamara Erickson, Ken Dychtwald, David Delong, Elisabeth Niejahr, and others that the upcoming workforce crisis is no joke and that few societies are preparing well to deal with it. To take just one aspect of this situation, consider the fact that birthrates in Japan, Germany, and Italy are roughly 1.2—so far below the replacement rate of 2.0 (the number of children that need to be born in order to replace the same number of people that die in a given country) that the Japanese government has developed increasingly more ambitious child-care centers and other benefits for working mothers in Japan in an effort to stem *shoshika*, a newly minted Japanese term that means "a society without children."[23] Elisabeth Niejahr's book on the topic is titled *Altenrepublik*, the "republic of the old."[24] Other countries with a birthrate below the replacement rate number are Canada, China, France, and the United Kingdom.

Although the workforce alarm bells are clanging, we think a significant slice of this situation is the need for developing greater numbers of leadership talent. Data abound concerning this issue. In 2003 the Center for Creative Leadership and *Chief Executive* showed that 78 percent of current leaders believed leadership development was either the most important or one of the top five most important factors for sustaining a competitive advantage.[25] During the thirteenth annual Asia Leadership Forum in 2004, held in Hong Kong, DNM-strategies and *BusinessWeek* showed that more than half of all leaders surveyed thought leadership was the most important factor for competitive success (more important than having the right business model or structures and processes) and that building leadership talent was the number one human resources issue.[26] And Development Dimensions International (DDI) found in their 2005–2006 Leadership Forecast study that roughly one-third of all internal leaders eventually fail because of poor people skills or poor interpersonal skills.[27] These are just samples of the numerous research reports that demonstrate the need for leadership development as an important focus of the overall need for talent and retention.

Contemporary Outcomes for Organizational Community

"THERE is no training to be a CEO; it's an extraordinary thing," said Gerald Levin, former CEO of AOL Time Warner. He told an audience at the Apollo Theater in New York that he would "fade away" as he left the CEO office and Richard Parsons took on the role.[28]

In one sense we can understand Mr. Levin's comment. CEO jobs are dramatically difficult, and 2002's Sarbanes-Oxley Act has made them even more difficult. Developing the skills and abilities to do the job well has frustrated more than one well-intentioned and well-rounded executive. Background, experience, education, and talent may not prepare you for the never-ending-on-public-display-globally-pressured-quarterly-earnings-report work that comes with leadership at the top. A study by the Center for Creative Leadership reports that 40 percent of CEOs fail during the first eighteen months of their tenure.[29] These odds plus the demands placed on a person in this position have caused a decided downturn in those who want to take on the pressure of the job. According to Harris Interactive, only about 35 percent of executives want the CEO position today, down from roughly half as many who aspired to it a mere four years ago.[30] Their research indicates that 60 percent of current executives do not want the job. Add this datum to the fact that CEO turnover is at a five-year high, and you have a problem: *who will lead companies in the future?*

Ask just about any leader whether he believes an important aspect of leadership responsibility is to develop other leaders, and he will easily affirm that this is a central responsibility. The next logical question to raise, then, is how to go about developing leaders. The three contemporary outcomes for this key part of the labor of leader-as-community-builder are explored below.

Fertile Environment

WE OPENED this book with a quote from BellSouth's Ron Frieson. We wish we had as many exemplars of BellSouth's devotion to development as we have clients, but unfortunately we do not. The truth is that some corporations have no leadership development practices; some have them, but senior executives are not involved; and only a small percentage of them have and institute such practices with sufficient executive involvement to make them work well.

Senior leaders who relegate leadership development solely to human resources deserve to be disappointed. This does not imply that human resources professionals or the human resources function is an inadequate system. What we do mean is that when it comes to leadership development, the impact of a senior leadership team's direct involvement should never be underestimated. It often makes the difference between mediocre and superior success.

Involvement includes, but is not necessarily limited to, showing up to kick off a course, event, or program. It can take the form of mentoring individual people. It can even take the form of teaching some portions of the course study. The presence and contribution of senior leaders is a type of "leader's touch" that cannot be achieved by proxy. In our experience, a senior leader kicking off a developmental session doubles the learning rate, which may have the effect of halving the cost outlay in terms of engagement and future performance.

In addition to individual senior managers being involved, the senior team must be united in their posture as to what type of leadership pipeline process is used. Having even one member who does not act in agreement with the process can have disruptive and detrimental effects upon the effort. GE's reputation for its leadership pipeline was not earned because it funded human resources; it was earned because serious leaders applied serious amounts of time to events, coaching, mentoring, teaching, and basically being visibly involved.

The best pipeline processes seem to be those that are separately created, separately funded activities, with serious involvement and oversight by the senior management team. When cost-reduction issues come into play, rather than cut leadership development expenses entirely, as some companies have been known to do, the better companies cut resources proportionally as they might with all other organizational needs.

Robust Development

The best developmental processes are earmarked by the following:

EXECUTIVE INVOLVEMENT

ROBUST CANDIDATE SELECTION

AGGRESSIVE TRAINING COMPONENTS

MENTORING AND/OR COACHING COMPONENTS

METRIC-BASED ASSESSMENTS FOR RESULTS COMPARISONS

STRATEGIC EXPERIENCES

While it is highly desirable to have all of these components, good results can still be achieved even when one or more of them is missing. But there is one component that is imperative for success, and that single, nonnegotiable element is executive involvement. We believe that *leadership development* is a good idea for all managers across the board, but such endeavors are expensive. Some people may view it as politically incorrect to select only a particular pool of candidates for inclusion to the process, but this is often the only way a good process can be funded. And once the decision is made, higher-ups must face tough choices as to which talented managers should be included. This decision making is no more difficult or impossible than many other resource choices executive teams must make. So make the best choices you can.

The biggest mistake we see senior leaders make is not creating a pipeline process that is by invitation only, but rather keeping the invitation list secret and often even attempting to keep the process secret. As in many endeavors of the modern world, transparency reigns. One aspect of transparency was noted by Jay Conger and Robert Fulmer in their research on how to marry succession planning systems and pipeline systems together:

> Succession planning systems have traditionally been shrouded in secrecy in an attempt to avoid sapping the motivation of those who aren't on the fast track... But given the fact that the employee contract is now based on performance—rather than loyalty or seniority—people will contribute more if they know what rung they are on.[31]

But it's not just letting candidates know where they stand that's important; it's also letting each of them know what's going on. We have provided training for leaders of high-potential programs who were not even told that the program they were selected for and instructed to attend was part of a leadership development process. Each time this happens, it is for the reason outlined above by Conger and Fulmer. Executives are afraid that others will resent the fact that a choice was made. Our straightforward advice: get over it.

The second biggest mistake we see leaders make is moving up extremely ambitious overachievers on the basis of performance alone. Using performance as the sole or most significant variable to determine a candidate's worthiness is shallow and holds potential dangers. A recent article detailing thirty-five years of study concerning achievement-oriented managers suggests: "In the short term, through sheer drive and determination, overachieving leaders may be very successful, but there's a dark side to the achievement motive. By relentlessly focusing on tasks and goals—revenue or sales targets, say—an executive or company can, over time, damage performance. Overachievers tend to command and coerce, rather than coach and collaborate, thus stifling subordinates."[32] Overachievers, by their very nature, may not be the best at leading self-managing teams; some research indicates that having the ability to empower and to persuade and build good relationships are keys for leaders who have such teams.[33]

Excess Talent

EMPLOYMENT choices abound, and talented managers have more organizational choices to exercise their abilities than ever before, which is part of the overall talent shortage. Executive temptation to simply use the outside supply of talent as a substitute for aggressive internal development has been increasingly frustrated as result. The bias that if you look outside closely enough, you can really snag the best may or may not be true, and even if this notion is true, it is not easy to apply.

One aspect of this bias has to do with CEO positions, perhaps the most important talent position to fill. Rakesh Khurana suggests in his book *Searching for a Corporate Savior* that looking outside for a CEO successor is part of a growing "irrational quest for charismatic chief executives."[34] He fears boards may be focusing too hard on the qualities of presence, personality, and media appeal rather than actual competence. He cites evidence that finding CEOs from outside has grown from 6 percent to 50 percent over the past several years. In a June 2003 *EIU Executive Briefing* article, he suggested the following guidelines for finding successors:

- Abandon hope for a corporate savior.

- Translate company strategy into operational terms.

- Identify skills required for key activities: activity/competency mapping.

- Assess internal candidates.

- Search for external candidates.

- Test and choose from short-list candidates.

- Calibrate goals, milestones, and compensation to drivers of success.[35]

Many researchers and practitioners have concluded that nurturing homegrown talent is best. When you cultivate internal talent, if you grow it well, you will have more than enough talent compared to opportunities. A *BusinessWeek* article about Schlumberger's deep talent resources told about a company that needed a country manager for Brazil. The company's human resources manager looked not just for a high-potential manager, but one who was mobile and could speak Portuguese. An initial search of the company's well-developed database yielded thirty-one candidates.[36]

This kind of surplus talent provides organizations with greater responsiveness to environmental changes. It can also yield frustration during slow growth times when high potentials are greater than opportunities. GE regularly spins off CEO potential managers as a result of its well-benchmarked leadership development process. Most of these managers don't complain, however. It seems that being qualified by GE improves a person's marketability. GE's process, as wonderful as it is, does not ensure future success, but it has certainly improved the odds.

Additional Thoughts on Community

THE BUZZ today seems centered on how the Internet is changing social practices, the way things get done, and basically all aspects of human endeavor. There is no doubt that the technological advance of the Internet and related technologies is having an amazing impact, but we are not certain we believe the hype that it is changing human nature as much as we believe it is providing human nature with a new and interesting method for expressing age-old phenomena.

Social networking Web sites like Facebook and MySpace command a great deal of media attention. YouTube and Flickr aren't so much huge watering holes, but rather gianormous (to use a contemporary word) bulletin boards that also seem to make the daily blog. But are these technological inventions dramatically changing the fact that people like to meet new people, feel popular, or look for convenience in connecting with others, or are they simply amplifying people's abilities to do these very human acts? We believe that not much has changed in terms of human behavior, but because we have dramatically changed our ability to engage in social behavior via technology, the manner in which organizations conceive of community is indeed changing.

Goldcorp, a Canadian gold-mining company, has made a historic entrance into the business case hall of fame with an unusual and daring use of the idea of community. The basic story is that Goldcorp had its financial back against the wall, and neither internal company experts nor external experts could figure out a good way to get more gold. Former CEO Rob McEwen posted the company's mining data on the Internet, offering a five-hundred-thousand-dollar incentive for anyone in the world who could help them find gold. A number of inventive and intelligent minds responded, most of whom Goldcorp would never have known to ask in the first place. This move led to Goldcorp's changing its fortunes through an imaginative use of community. Don Tapscott and Anthony Williams use an expanded version of this story to advance their idea of "wikinomics" in their book *Wikinomics: How Mass Collaboration Changes Everything.*[37]

Large-scale community collaborations are seen as the wave of the future, and there is a certain amount of evidence that the technology-enabled, globally invited communities may provide many types of organizations with opportunities to participate in new forums. One the one hand, stories like Goldcorp stimulate the imagination to consider expanded community ideas. On the other, the incident just seems like a modern-day version of running a full-page ad in the *Times* (London or New York) posting a reward. Technology helps with this type of community collaboration, but does the new process replace the sense of community most of us experience when working with a dedicated set of known colleagues working on a project, issue, or need that truly engages? The colleagues might share late-night pizzas with us literally in a garage start-up or simply share a videoconference line used on a weekly basis, but what binds them is a shared sense of working together.

The issue we believe leaders face in terms of collaboration, technology, and community has to do with a sense of communal spirit. Regardless of methodology, leaders need to establish a sense of communion and forge a bond that joins people together to share in a common purpose and enables them to feel part of a whole.

6 *Case Studies*

THE FOLLOWING three case studies showcase the integration model. Both individual and organizational leadership forces shaped the organizations depicted here. One organization no longer exists. Two exist in some degree as they were initially shaped, each having undergone some changes. At the end of each case, we comment on the individual and organizational leadership tensions of the primary leader.

Andrew Higgins: Wall Buster

ANDREW HIGGINS was born on August 28, 1886, the youngest of ten children.[1] During the 1870s, his father, John, had been a newspaper reporter for the *Chicago Times* and later became a partner in a Chicago law firm. While living through the recessionary cycles of the 1870s and 1880s, John dreamed of having his own law practice in California. With his wife, Annie O'Conner Higgins, and children, he left Chicago one day and headed west. Along this journey he was asked by his former newspaper editor to interview the retired Indian scout Major Frank North, who lived in Columbus, Nebraska. The interview resulted in his staying long enough for his California dream to dissipate. The countryside of the Loup and Platt Rivers and the friendliness of the citizens he encountered charmed his soul. He persuaded his wife to stay and eventually became a judge.

Annie moved the family to Omaha, Nebraska, during the early 1890s after her husband died of injuries sustained falling down stairs. Andrew was seven at the time, and his natural independence, curiosity, and ability were likely stimulated through the complications of losing a father and relocating. His entrepreneurial spirit seized opportunities soon after the move. He started cutting neighbors' grass with a hand sickle when he was nine, but soon his organizing talent and ambition led him to start hiring other boys to work under him. To accelerate their efforts, he upgraded his equipment to lawnmowers. He supervised their work and sold new customers on the reliability of his grass-mowing gang. As the enterprise grew, he wondered what other business opportunities his neighborhood had to offer. Before long he started organizing the delivery routes for the *Omaha Daily News*, which later included selling subscriptions and collecting payments. Again he quickly hired others to distribute while he built up the business. He was earning one hundred dollars per month by 1898 and soon sold his newspaper business to an adult for seventeen hundred dollars. Not bad for a twelve-year-old kid, who was earning more than many adults at the end of a long recessionary period. At the time, rental properties for couples or small families ranged from ten to thirty dollars per month, and many adults had difficulty finding steady full-time employment.

The young Higgins traded a small portion of his earnings for a wrecked sailboat and rebuilt it, the genesis of a lifelong love of boats. But he found that water sailing wasn't fast enough for him. Try as he might, he could not get enough speed from sailing on water. So he switched surfaces and prototyped a design for an ice-sailing boat, hoping this would help him reach a speed that would hold his interest. His ingenuity and resolve presented itself in full force in the summer of 1898 when he built his first iceboat in his mother's basement. When it was completed, he had to remove it from the house. Waiting until his mother was away for the day, he collected some of his friends and former employees, removed enough of a brick wall section from the basement to ease the boat out, and, as best he could, restored the wall—all before his mother returned home. It is not clear whether Andrew had planned this all along, since it was warmer in the basement than outside, or if he simply didn't allow a "ship in a bottle" type of problem to stand in his way.

Racing his iceboat at roughly sixty miles an hour thrilled him, but as with many inventors, entrepreneurs, and future CEOs, school didn't. He didn't like the scholastic work and had reported difficulties with authority figures. His mother, however, had instilled in him a love of reading and thinking on his own, an interest and ability that shaped his approach to life. His disquiet at school led him to join the Nebraska National Guard, where he was introduced to amphibious landings along the Platte River. That experience, absorbing a dozen or so books on military history, and developing a fascination and admiration for John Paul Jones were instrumental stimulations that sparked an extraordinary life.

Higgins's childhood talents for organizing work and selling customers developed into full-fledged leadership skills that touched his every endeavor. As a sergeant major in the National Guard, his team won most contests they entered. After his discharge, he drove a delivery truck and became a superintendent for M. E. Smith and Company, a dry goods concern, which doubled its growth during his two-year sojourn with them. His love of boats and the money he saved during this period allowed Higgins to leave the great American plains to be near the water, and he made Mobile, Alabama, his home. Shortly after arriving, he began to cast about for an opportunity to use his commercial abilities. He decided to take a three-month course on farming and amazed generational farmers with his high-yield crops within his first and second seasons. He was so successful that he reinvested his savings by purchasing forested land adjacent to his farm and setting up a sawmill. He was not quite twenty years old.

By 1909 Andrew had married, seen the birth of his first son, and determined to become a lumber exporter. He had learned from experience how to make lumber profitable, and the business would also allow him to enjoy his boat-building hobby. To equip himself for his future enterprise, he educated himself by taking jobs as a lading clerk for a steamship company and as a foreign exchange banker, and working in several positions within the timber industry, including estimator, buyer, and inspector. He held each position long enough to thoroughly understand how each worked and how they all worked together.

He relocated after graduating from his "schooling" to New Orleans and in 1910 began employment with a lumber house, where his skills as an organizer helped him reach the position of general manager. As the early hostilities of World War I began to break in Europe, he realized the timing was right to launch his own enterprise, and with two other partners he opened A. J. Higgins Lumber and Export Company. His business prospered through the increased lumber consumption that the war fueled. Turning thirty in 1916, his dynamic personality and commercial prowess was hitting stride. In his biography of Higgins, *Andrew Jackson Higgins and the Boats That*

Won World War II, Jerry E. Strahan provides a description of Higgins at this point in his life.

> He was strong and rugged, but his face projected a boyish appearance. The appearance was deceiving, as beneath the youthful face was an impatient, never-accept-"no" individual with an explosive Irish temper. Also beneath the innocent face was a talented salesman, a great storyteller, and a man of remarkable charisma.

Higgins built a successful business and was enjoying the pleasure boats he built and sold. As his business grew, he looked for talent to add to his enterprise. He tended to not like university-educated engineers, but instead looked for hands-on tinkerers and others who could create prototypes. It wasn't just raw skill or aptitude that interested him, though. He wanted his engineers to possess some curiosity or creativity as well as technical ability but believed that engineering schools only taught a person what they *couldn't* do. He doubted that engineering school doused engineers' belief in possibility. Higgins wanted men who had learned what they *could* do. He also bucked the tradition of the day and hired many blacks and women, paying them on the same wage scale as their white male counterparts. To him, work ability made you an equal, and nothing much else mattered. While this was a progressive posture and gained him a loyal and hardworking workforce, other parts of his temperament led to commercial problems. He was an outspoken, hot-tempered man, who hated bureaucratic red tape, loved bourbon, and saw many obstacles as simply another basement wall that had to be knocked down. Sometimes the walls he knocked through were other people's egos.

In 1930 the U.S. Navy and Marine Corps changed warfare strategies; they began looking for better landing craft and turned to the big boat companies of the Eastern seaboard for solutions. Higgins believed he could compete with larger, experienced naval boat builders and gained the navy's attention by competing in a competition for "plywood derby" prototype landing craft sponsored by the navy. His fresh approach to the problem prompted the navy to ask if Higgins would look at their designs. Higgins agreed, and according to the June 6, 1994, edition of *Time* magazine, he responded in his characteristic manner.

He scrawled across their plan, "This is lousy." Higgins had a better idea for a light, maneuverable boat with a protected propeller that did not easily foul in the shallows. "Show us," said the Navy. Higgins took over an entire block of New Orleans' Polyminia Street, set up floodlights, put machines and people to work around the clock. Fourteen days later, with the last paint applied as the freight flatcars clacked east, nine Higgins boats rolled into Norfolk, Virginia.

By 1940 Higgins was producing workboats and prototype landing craft. His arrogance annoyed the navy's Bureau of Ships, which favored the big Eastern-seaboard shipyards. But when America entered the Second World War, the bureau's annoyance softened as the men who fought many battles in all theaters of war praised Higgins's boat-building genius and considered him a godsend.

"Higgins boats" was the common name attached to the LCVP (Land Craft Vehicle Personnel) that he and his crew of engineers designed and refined. They gave the military the ability to transport thousands of men and hundreds of tons of equipment swiftly through the surf to less-fortified beaches, eliminating the need for established harbors. Not only could the boat beach itself where other boats were unable to, but it could also unbeach itself. The Allies no longer had to sweep harbors of mines and commandeer enemy-held ports before they could land an assault force. The new craft allowed Allied commanders to conceive and implement warfare strategies that were inconceivable before the Higgins boats.

Higgins operated eight separate plants, employing more than 20,000 workers. Peak output exceeded 700 boats a month. His total output for the Allies during World War II was 20,094. Higgins Industries received both the army's and the navy's highest awards for production and quality on several occasions. At one point, more than 90 percent of all boats used to transport troops were built by Higgins Industries. Historian Stephen E. Ambrose, whose *D-Day June 6, 1944: The Climactic Battle of World War II* was the basis of Steven Spielberg's *Saving Private Ryan*, wrote the following about Higgins:

> Once he got the initial contract, Higgins showed that he was as much a genius at mass production as he was at design. He had assembly lines scattered throughout New Orleans (some under canvas). He employed, at the peak, 30,000 workers. It was an integrated work force of blacks,

women, and men, the first ever in New Orleans. Higgins inspired his workers the way a general tries to inspire his troops. A huge sign hung over one of his assembly lines: "The Man Who Relaxes Is Helping the Axis." He put pictures of Hitler, Mussolini, and Hirohito sitting on toilets in his factory bathrooms. "Come on in, brother," the caption read. "Take it easy. Every minute you loaf here helps us plenty."

Higgins's strength of character, his ambition to win, his ability to organize and inspire, his execution bias, his hatred of bureaucracy, and his love of design and rapid prototyping seem like the modern-day competencies many global companies seek in their CEOs. His prowess even impressed Hitler, who dubbed him the "new Noah." Ambrose interviewed Dwight D. Eisenhower in 1964 and was astonished when Ike said: "Andrew Higgins won the war for us. If Higgins had not designed and built those LCVPs, we never could have landed over an open beach. The whole strategy of the war would have been different."

The massive production contracts of World War II made Higgins's strengths—design and rapid production—very important. Administrative weaknesses were suddenly irrelevant. War offered him opportunity. Had the Japanese not bombed Pearl Harbor, Higgins probably would have remained a successful, but small, Southern boat builder. Andrew Jackson Higgins died on August 1, 1952, and was buried in Metairie Cemetery just outside of New Orleans.

In 1999 a group working with the National D-day Museum in New Orleans built a Higgins boat with the combined volunteer efforts of a variety of people who were drawn to what was known as the Higgins Boat Project. The boat was built with materials and plans of the World War II era. In fact, during the year the boat was built, Lloyd Lovitt had been contacted to inspect the 1999 Higgins boat. He had been the U.S. Navy Bureau of Ships inspector assigned to Higgins Industries during the war. Mr. Lovitt's review: "That boat is in every way representative of the quality of construction that I saw at Higgins Industries during WW II."

The author of the last Higgins Boat Project newsletter, Jimmy Duckworth, described his personal experience while on the Higgins boat the project team had built.

I found the boat to be very powerful. It leapt very quickly from dead in the water to sea speed. You could easily feel the power. In addition to having a tough reputation, this boat had JUICE!!! I know some veteran coxswains reading this are smiling as they remember running the boat, but most Americans haven't had the opportunity. In short, when you're holding the helm and throttle of a Higgins boat, you feel like you've GOT something!

On November 6, 1999, Gayle Higgins Jones, Andrew Higgins's daughter, dedicated the boat by grasping a bottle of Old Grand-Dad bourbon and announcing, "I christen thee U.S. Coast Guard PA33-21, in honor of all the men who saw combat in one of your 20,000 predecessors." She smashed the bottle against the boat, and the distinct bourbon bouquet complemented the thunderous applause. It wasn't until later that those who had been involved in the project were notified that Lloyd Lovitt had passed away in his Tennessee home during the evening of the christening.

Analysis

THIS case study demonstrates how crisis calls upon the strength and resolve of a generation and how a gifted individual leader can respond. Individual authenticity was never a problem with Higgins. Everyone knew exactly where they stood with him, including high-ranking government officials. His engineering competence, ability to inspire commitment and confidence, and his basic honest and direct work ethic won him many a loyal follower. For the short-term duration of the war, his ability to innovate and build an organization to produce new ideas was literally amazing. His skill at short-term navigation held him in good stead. He was able to build a dedicated community through his own brand of engagement practices and in many respects was ahead of his time in terms of honoring diversity.

Yet his postwar leadership skills were not equally impressive. Without an emergency to draw upon his talents, he was unable to rethink his organizational strategy. His tenderness for people was a hallmark of his individual leadership skills, but his inability to resize and restructure his organization failed him. In short, his abilities as an individual leader across all four labors were highly admirable, and during the period building up to and just before the war he was able to build a small and engaging organization. But his organizational leadership skills were not sufficiently strong, especially in the areas of community, navigation, and architecture, to allow him to return to commercial viability. Because his ailing company could not survive, leadership succession had no soil in which to root. Higgins deserves recognition for his mark on history and his contribution to the times in which he lived, and it is regrettable that he could not grow an organization that succeeded his own personal greatness.

Mary Kay Ash: Practical Idealist

FROM THE early 1800s to recent times, a variety of hot sulfuric springs around the United States have attracted visitors with their medicinal and therapeutic benefits. Many people believe that bodily emersion into these hot springs creates osmotic exchanges that relieve rheumatism, arthritis, and a variety of skin diseases and other ailments. Several of these historic locations can be found across southern Texas. Sam Houston reportedly bathed his wounds at Sour Lake, Texas. Davy Crockett dipped his celebrated soul in springs close to Sour Wells, Texas. In the early 1900s, Mineral Wells, Texas, hosted as many as 150,000 visitors annually. Some of its celebrity visitors included Clark Gable, Tom Mix, Douglas Fairbanks, and J. P. Morgan. The merchants of this 8,000-resident town were surely pleased. And in 1915 in Hot Wells, Texas, a young woman was born who would become a celebrated entrepreneur.[2]

Mary Kay Ash's life started hard. Her father had tuberculosis, and at age six she started caring for him while her mother worked fourteen-hour days at a restaurant. During this tender developmental period, she learned from her mother a "you can do anything" mantra that stayed with her all of her life. Mary Kay married young and had three children with her first husband. To help support her family during the latter part of the Great Depression, she accepted a challenge from a door-to-door encyclopedia salesman to sell ten sets of encyclopedias in one month. The sales rep told her that if she could make this standard quota, she would earn one free set. She sold all ten in two days.

In 1939 she became a sales representative for the Stanley Home Products Company. Her experience there contributed to her business understanding, which she was able to use later when she started her own company. The Stanley company had been founded by Frank Stanley Beveridge and Catherine L. O'Brien in 1931. Frank had met Catherine while they both worked at the innovative and highly successful Fuller Brush Company. He was a vice president and she was an associate, but they dreamed of owning a business that would create an opportunity for people during the Depression to start their own businesses without the need for much start-up capital. This dream, coupled with their Fuller Brush Company experience, shaped Stanley Home Products, a door-to-door-selling company offering household cleaners, brushes, and mops.

About the same time that Mary Kay joined the company, an imaginative Stanley dealer, who had experimented with giving product demonstrations to clubs and organizations to increase sales volume, related his experience to other Stanley dealers. His initial experiment evolved into a home-based selling process that became known as the "party plan." Catherine L. O'Brien went on to become president, and later chairwoman, of Stanley Home Products, a career development that did not escape Mary Kay's notice.

Mary Kay learned many valuable lessons during her time with Stanley. Three weeks after joining she attended an annual convention in Dallas where that year's Queen of Sales was awarded an alligator handbag. This impressed Mary Kay to the extent that she set out to earn the Queen of Sales award the following year. She succeeded, but was awarded a trophy instead of the handbag she wanted. Disappointed with a mere statue, she purchased and carried a gold-initialed alligator briefcase. Her continuing sales success enabled Mary Kay and her husband to move out of her mother's house into their own home.

Mary Kay evidently believed that increasing knowledge and competence were important steps to self-improvement, so she started taking premed classes at the University of Houston. Her ambitions were dreadfully interrupted when her husband divorced her upon his return from World War II. She rallied from this setback by enlisting her three children to pack products and began full-time work for Stanley. Her son Richard later became her business partner and CEO of Mary Kay Cosmetics.

At Stanley, Mary Kay was a talented recruiter and marketer, but she was unsuccessful in being promoted to unit manager, something she felt she had earned. Frustrated by the company's male orientation and lack of recognition of her ideas, she left Stanley in 1952 and started working for World Gift Company, a Dallas home accessories firm. She started as national training director and during her tenure there was instrumental in extending distribution to forty-three states. As a result of her hard and often inventive work, she became a member of the board of directors. Just as it seemed she was in line for a job that would recognize her accomplishments, however, a young man she had earlier trained was promoted above her, at twice her salary. That event, along with the board's dismissal of many of her ideas, was the final straw, and she quit the company in 1963, at a time when women's' rights issues began to ignite across the United States.

In characteristic fashion, Mary Kay reflected upon her experiences and began a detailed listing of all she had learned about selling and building a business from her already successful career. She considered putting her ideas together in a book that described a dream company in which women would be empowered, not limited in earnings potential, not bounded by "glass ceilings" (a term that came into popularity long after Mary Kay had bruised her head on it several times). But during the writing process, it occurred to her overachieving spirit that it would be more fun to build a company that exemplified the dream than to just dream and write about it.

This reflective period had helped her sort out her business plan. She realized she knew how to build a successful sales organization, but she lacked a product. She didn't have to look far to find one. She had been using a skin softener for some time made by a local hide tanner. She approached the hide tanner's daughter, purchased the formulas, and turned them into a line of skin cream products. This was something she thought women could relate to and would need to replenish on a regular basis.

Her second husband handled many of the financial affairs as she put together a recruiting and sales plan. But just as they were about to launch the company, he died of a heart attack. The accountant and legal experts they had consulted were concerned that Mary Kay couldn't handle the business without her husband and suggested she abandon her dream. Ignoring their advice, she launched the company one month later on a dreaded Friday the thirteenth, defying men and superstition to stop her. The company was named Beauty and occupied downtown Dallas retail space. Her son Richard Rogers quit his job in Houston and returned home to join the start-up. Determined to leverage her selling experience and her developed sense of empowering women to succeed, she began recruiting. She trained nine saleswomen in her door-to-door method, but quickly realized that her forty-hour-workweek system wasn't suitable for women who wanted a flexible work life that allowed them to work and maintain a family. She returned to the home-party selling method, adding a few special inventions of her own, and the Mary Kay Cosmetics franchise model began to grow.

Mary Kay educated her sales force with very specific, personally learned and valued selling techniques. She taught them to be "Beauty Consultants," not saleswomen, and stressed that while each of them ran their own business, they were all in business together. The memories of her alligator bag and other lost rewards fueled her distinctive reward and recognition programs that included the now-famous pink Cadillacs, vacations, diamond rings, and bumblebee brooches. "Mary Kay pink" extended to include the color of its fleet of eighteen-wheeler distribution trucks and has become synonymous with the company and its founder, who once owned a pink mansion.

For Mary Kay, product sales were important, but they were largely a means to an end: enriching and empowering women's lives. One of her most often repeated ideas was: "Don't limit yourself. Many people limit themselves to what they think they can do. You can go as far as your mind lets you. What you believe, remember, you can achieve." She later formulized her thoughts into nine leadership values that permeated the Mary Kay Cosmetics company during her lifetime. These values were:

- Create and maintain a common brand
- Create the future: think and act strategically

- Make employees feel important

- Motivate others with recognition and celebration

- Never leave your values

- Innovate or evaporate

- Foster balance

- Have a higher purpose

- OK never does it: you've got to be great

Her third husband, Mel Ash, died of cancer in 1980, and Mary Kay committed to fighting the disease and finding a cure. She raised a great deal of money for research, and in 1996 established the Mary Kay Ash Charitable Foundation, a nonprofit public foundation that funds research into cancers affecting women. She twice served as the honorary chair of the Texas Breast Cancer Screening Project. She lobbied the Texas legislature to require insurance companies to cover mammograms and applied her persuasive talents for many cancer organizations.

Mary Kay died on Thanksgiving Day, 2001. Rubye Lee-Mills, Independent National Sales Director Emeritus, said, "I don't think there will ever be another woman who believes in women the way Mary Kay did." In 2003 Mary Kay Cosmetics' revenue reached more than $1.8 billion in wholesale sales. According to the Mary Kay Web site, as of October 2005, 1.3 million Independent Beauty Consultants were enjoying their own businesses in more than thirty markets worldwide.

Analysis

THE ASH and Higgins stories bear some resemblance. Born into demanding, even harsh, life conditions, Ash, too, rose above her personal early circumstances through sheer willpower and personality. She was industrious and studious, which prompted her intense desire to succeed in business as a woman. Her lifelong drive to free women from the social limitations of her generation is laudable, and for many women she is a true hero.

Mary Kay possessed individual leadership abilities in abundance. She was able to attract, engage, and retain talent, and her personal charisma was instrumental in creating a successful following. Her navigational goals and ability to focus on profitable strategies to achieve them worked well. Over time, she took the general home-party selling system and applied a special Mary Kay sense of innovation to it.

However, many people believe that the system, fashioned during a different age of women in the workplace, has not evolved with the times. Some even suggest that the principles instilled in Mary Kay representatives are inflexible and create a type of false enthusiasm and robotic behavior. Mary Kay seemed less able to adapt to changing times than to continue to relive the times in which her leadership abilities were forged. Other organizations, such as Avon, have surpassed Mary Kay's size and market penetration. While there is still room for the home-party selling method in modern society, the Mary Kay organization innovates slowly in this regard. Moreover, it seems Mary Kay was more interested in developing great saleswomen than in developing any quality leadership succession plan. She was highly admired as an individual leader across all four labors and showed some promise in her organizational authenticity abilities. But she left her organization with less ability to navigationally adapt or create a new dynamic organization design.

Akio Morita: Tradition Breaker

MOST Japanese cities were badly damaged during the Second World War. Tokyo had lost 60 percent of its buildings, and 30 percent of Japan's industrial capacity was destroyed. Millions of soldiers and civilians joined their friends and families on an overcrowded and suffering mainland after leaving territories Japan had been forced to relinquish at the end of the war. Many traditional-minded senior military leaders committed ritual suicide. Lives were destroyed, and the stain of defeat competed with, and was often overpowered by, the need for basic shelter and food. It is difficult for Americans to comprehend the depth of Japan's devastation; Europeans are far better able to understand life after ruin.

From the rubble, many hardworking Japanese went back to work to rebuild their cities and continue their enterprises, just as the men and women in Europe did. People in all countries sought to restore a sense of cultural and national pride and to overcome their shame or sorrow. It was a time of great change and challenge to tradition. One person who challenged tradition was Akio Morita, who was born in Nagoya, a port city located halfway between Tokyo and Kyoto that had lost most of its industrial and historic buildings during the war.[3] His family had brewed sake for more than three centuries, and his father, Kyuzaemon, had adhered to time-honored, traditional standards to prepare his son to become head of the family business. Akio learned about business and engineering from an early age, both by working in the family business, even during school holidays, and by disassembling and reassembling every novel gadget his well-to-do family could afford.

This slightly built man with bluish eyes, a rare trait among Japanese, graduated from the physics department at Osaka Imperial University in 1944. For the last period of the war he served as a lieutenant in the Imperial Navy and was a member of its Wartime Research Committee, where he first met his future business partner, Masaru Ibuka. Ibuka and Morita initially connected through their interest in engineering. During the final months of the war, they considered what would happen upon its conclusion. They longed to turn their talents away from waging war and toward building great products. Their meeting would lead to a major change both in Morita's life and in the postwar view of Japan.

On May 7, 1946, Ibuka and Morita founded Tokyo Tsushin Kogyo K. K. (Tokyo Telecommunications Engineering Corporation) with fewer than two dozen employees and a modest capitalization. Ibuka was thirty-eight years old and Morita was twenty-five. The two men were the rarest of business partners in that they never quarreled in public, remained devoted to each other throughout their career, and often were thought of as inseparable. From the beginning they generally divided their energies. Ibuka handled technological research and product development, and Morita focused on marketing, globalization, finance, and human resources. It proved to be an optimum split of talent, and in many ways was typical of how business founders become successful.

Morita traded away the relative certainties of comfort and privilege during a time when few people enjoyed any comfort, and yoked his entrepreneurial spirit to an ambitious idea. It seems in retrospect that Morita wanted to *make* a mark rather than inherit one. It was the first of many major departures from tradition that Morita would make over the course of his life.

It is easy to associate Morita with Sony's famous brand and its varied successes and challenges today. But in the early days before the company name changed, things weren't always so glamorous. At first he and Ibuka purchased a Datsun truck for one hundred dollars on the black market and loaded and unloaded supplies themselves. They tried to sell an electric rice cooker, but the product's adoption rate was slowed by tradition and poor electrical infrastructure, as well as a manufacturing problem or two. Another of their first electronic gadgets didn't fare well, either. Imagine a tape recorder roughly the size of a small microwave oven that weighed seventy-five pounds and was expensive to boot, and you can understand some of the start-up difficulties the fledgling company encountered in a country battling to regain a measure of itself.

One of Morita's great advantages, however, was a lack of local Japanese corporate identity. Postwar Japan was being rebuilt by giant companies like Toshiba, Mitsubishi, and Hitachi that controlled the basic steel-making and manufacturing industry at the time. This situation provided Morita with another first. He realized that the only way he could build a great company was by marketing to the rest of the world, that Japan was too wrecked by war and too eager to seek support from known local name brands. Although at first he remained traditional-minded and focused only upon Japan, he finally explored territory that many of his business colleagues would have considered dangerous if not actually disrespectful to Japanese tradition. Once his mind turned to the world marketplace, he began his journey of pursuing the world beyond Japan both physically and psychologically.

Several events molded Morita's resolve, and one story from his 1999 *Economist* obituary deserves recounting. Morita started traveling the world to understand different cultures and to maintain close contact with scientists and engineers about the latest ideas and technologies. In the 1950s a Düsseldorf waiter served him a bowl of ice cream decorated with a miniature parasol from Japan. It's likely that the waiter was merely trying to be friendly and making a gesture for his guest, but the symbolic nature of the interchange struck a deep chord for Morita. Events such as these built a tsunami of resolve within Morita's mind to reverse the world's image of Japan as a country of trinkets and cheap reproductions and make people see it instead as one spoke of innovation, originality, and quality.

Another significant first for Morita and Ibuka was their decision to rename the company. Morita had determined that America was going to play a major role in their future success, and they wanted a company name that was short, easy to pronounce, and easy to remember, a name that any brand agency would love to market. They pored through dictionaries looking for words that would work, and when they found the Latin word *sonus*, for "sound," legend has it that several symbolic tumblers clicked in their minds. *Sonus* and *sound* were simple words, and the pop term *sonny boys* was often used in America at the time to refer to whiz kids or youthful energy. Thus the name "Sony" was conceived. In another break from tradition, Morita decided to write the new company name in *katakana*, a Japanese alphabet that is normally used to write foreign names, something that was unheard of at that time.

Morita's boundless energy and devotion to exploring the world market led him to one new idea after another. He moved his family to New York to immerse himself in American culture. Against the advice of others, he insisted that the Sony "Walkman" carry the same name worldwide. His advisers around the globe had wanted to use different names for the product to suit their national markets: "Soundabout" in the United States, "Freestyle" in Sweden, and in Britain, "Stowaway." It's difficult to imagine now that any of those terms would have survived like "Walkman." During a time when Japanese businesses borrowed money only from the Japanese banks they relied upon, Sony was the first company to issue American Depositary Receipts and offer shares on the New York Stock Exchange. Raising capital from outside Japan was considered outrageous by some of Morita's contemporaries.

As his excursions into nontraditional, international territory grew, so did his vision of the world. He was among the first to use terms like "Think globally, act locally" anywhere, especially in Japan. The renowned author of business strategy Keniche Ohmae was inspired by Morita to use the phrase in his book *The Borderless World*. And perhaps most significantly, Morita's undying love for the newest in science led him and Ibuka to William Shockley at Bell Labs shortly after the birth of the transistor. In 1953 they paid twenty-five thousand dollars to license the technology, and four years later Sony's transistor radios were enabling millions of rock-and-roll-crazed, teenaged baby boomers to tune in to their favorite DJs and songs. Sony and sound entered the mainstream.

While the company enjoyed huge hits, like the Walkman, and suffered huge setbacks, like the Betamax, it seemed that Morita's energy was never depleted. As Sony's brand reputation grew, he reached for more. Over the years, Morita's personality seemed to develop a dual nature. Torn between his traditional upbringing and his unbelievable success at breaking tradition, to many he seemed to have two faces. For example, he disinherited his eldest son, Hideo Morita, for marrying without his consent. It is difficult to imagine an act of this nature from a man who had once disobeyed his own father's wishes. His immediate family witnessed his consummate international business "performance," but few outside the family saw the private side of his personality.

Morita played as hard as he worked. A sports enthusiast, he learned to wind surf, scuba, and ski in his fifties and sixties. He loved music, art, and politics and became friends with Kiichi Miyazawa, former prime minister of Japan; Henry Kissinger, former U.S. Secretary of State; and orchestra conductors Zubin Mehta and Herbert von Karajan.

Morita suffered a cerebral hemorrhage five years before he passed away on October 3, 1999. He received many prestigious awards during his lifetime from a variety of world governments. Upon Morita's death, former Japanese prime minister Keizo Obuchi, remarked that Morita had been "the engine that pulled the Japanese economy." Keniche Ohmae, in his tribute to Morita, wrote, "The great tragedy is that Japan does not have another like him."

Analysis

MORITA was clearly gifted as an individual leader. He was able to gain, engage, and retain commitment; created an organization that is a model of innovative culture; had a rare navigational ability to see far beyond the boundaries of tradition; and was courageous enough to find business structures that allowed him to realize his dreams.

As an organizational leader, Morita was adaptive and certainly authentically minded. But it seems his internal need to always innovate led his organization to develop "the Sony way" muscles to the detriment of building other organizational capabilities. The current Blu-ray versus HD competition seems all too similar to the Betamax versus VHS technology race of a previous generation. The organization may not be considered by many to have "dynamic design" in mind as it continues its Sony-minded innovation. And it does not appear that Morita imbued Sony with any ability to develop leaders that could take the helm of this radically different Japanese company, which has led Sony to default to traditional succession practices or look for senior leadership change from the outside. No leader since his passing has been able to keep the company growing or healthy in the way he did.

Case Study Summary

THESE three case studies outline three different, legendary leaders: people whose work reshaped the experience and lives of countless constituents—and, in at least one case, literally saved lives. These short studies highlight the struggle and saga of these three people's lives, and we do not pretend they are full biographies that contain detailed blow-by-blow analysis, replete with financial charts and graphs. We do, however, believe that these brief overviews describe the general major themes each leader faced and their reaction to it. In all three cases, these leaders exerted their experienced, tested talents against great causes and obtained honorable and noteworthy results. We suspect there are many people who would claim that their lives were changed during their tenure in the three organizations discussed above. We further imagine many would say their leader was admired and beloved.

We chose these examples because during their lifetimes all three leaders were held in high esteem, underwent a period of developmental experiences that tempered their resolve to do something great, and were highly successful. All of these factors make for the kind of leadership case studies we most enjoy reading and recounting.

We also chose these three examples to illustrate the differences between individual leadership and organizational leadership. Higgins, Ash, and Morita were admired, respected, and followed by those who accepted their leadership, despite flaws that all leaders have. They built successful organizations, including two that survive today. And all three case studies allow us to examine and consider how acts of individual leadership do not necessarily qualify as acts of organizational leadership; like not seeing the forest past the towering redwood in front of you, it is sometimes difficult to truly see an organization past its leader.

In each of these cases the leaders were authentic to the core. Higgins's brash confidence, willingness to fight against discrimination, and boisterous demeanor combined with his natural engineering genius to forge a "man's man" in a dark age that needed inspiration's light to pierce the darkness of tyranny. Ash's "over-achiever" personality was fueled by her passionate belief that women were not second class and could be independent business leaders if given a method and support. Morita's fierce independence, daring and reckless spirit, and his nearly unimaginable divorce from tradition provided him with the opportunity to literally go where no Japanese leader had ever gone before.

Yet each of these successful leaders also failed in some measure at organizational leadership. That they were each effective leaders we do not question. In fact, we think they were terrific and would be considered inspirational individual leaders by almost everyone. Whether or not they were successful organizational leaders, however, we leave to you to analyze, as we have done.

7 *From Individual Success to Organization Significance*

As the first president of the United States, George Washington earned a prominent place in history and history books.[1] Many legendary stories of his life, work, and posture exist, but the following facts about him are undisputed.

- Born in Virginia
- Lost his father when he was eleven
- Became a surveyor
- Educated himself in military science
- Served with distinction and increasing military rank with the Virginia militia during the French and Indian Wars and in various other military engagements before the Revolutionary War
- Spent more than two decades as a gentleman farmer before becoming president
- Became interested in the growing conflicts with England
- Participated in the early Continental Congresses
- Joined in the Revolutionary War and eventually became commander of all the colonial forces
- Quelled a short-lived rally by some of his supporters to appoint him king of the colonies
- Served two terms as the first U.S. president and then decided to retire and not run for a third term

Many historians suggest that Washington's greatest talent—above even his military ability—was holding together a struggling, fractionalized new organization, the United States of America, as a great number of deep-thinking, highly articulate leaders competed to have their worldviews dominate the political ideology of that formative era.

137

His presidential farewell address is long and aptly dressed in the political ornamentation of its time, yet there are passages that reveal Washington's thoughts and feelings about his leadership ability and legacy in a direct manner. Of his leadership ability, he said: "The impressions with which I first undertook the arduous trust were explained on the proper occasion. In the discharge of this trust, I will only say that I have, with good intentions, contributed towards the organization and administration of the government the best exertions of which a very fallible judgment was capable."

Washington always accepted huge responsibility with a humility that earned him respect and trust, even from his detractors. His personal motives to improve the colony's ability to engage in commerce merged with his developed social interests to create a governmental body that could prosper without a distant controlling sovereign. His military instincts, bolstered by personal courage and boldness, were amplified by his ability to understand the larger picture. During the Revolutionary War, Washington believed one big battle would end the conflict that had resulted from the decades of disagreement. His alliance with France allowed him to defeat Cornwallis, also an energetic and courageous field general, at the significant Battle of Yorktown. And it was this battle that unraveled the British Parliament's resolve to continue the war.

While serving as president, rather than place people of his own political persuasion in powerful positions, Washington allowed a good deal of opposing thought to weigh in and appointed both Alexander Hamilton and Thomas Jefferson to his cabinet. A more extreme example of intentionally introduced tension is hard to find, as these two towering leaders fought passionately for their opposing ideologies. Washington was generally distrustful of partisan politics, and though he was disappointed that political parties gained strength and shape during his tenure, he worked to ensure that his position was as fair and committed to the overall cause as possible. His personal authenticity was one of his most admired characteristics.

Washington's farewell address stated a central idea that all political party members could agree upon: "Interwoven as is the love of liberty with every ligament of your hearts, no recommendation of mine is necessary to fortify or confirm the attachment." But in this most obvious, yet most necessary, reminder of the essence of gaining independence, he warned the main political camps that flowed from the Hamilton-Jefferson division to remember that internal conflicts were as dangerous to the newfound freedom and organizational structure as external threats. He admonished all competing idealists to consider that:

> it is of infinite moment that you should properly estimate the immense value of your national union to your collective and individual happiness; that you should cherish a cordial, habitual, and immovable attachment to it; accustoming yourselves to think and speak of it as of the palladium of your political safety and prosperity; watching for its preservation with jealous anxiety; discountenancing whatever may suggest even a suspicion that it can in any event be abandoned; and indignantly frowning upon the first dawning of every attempt to alienate any portion of our country from the rest, or to enfeeble the sacred ties which now link together the various parts.

Washington's leadership reminds us all that the individual and the collective can be united in a common cause. In the final sections of the address, he declares that his "predominate motive" was to help a young nation settle its bid for freedom and have enough time free from conflict to mature and grow the ability to sustain itself and reap the fortunes of its own efforts.

This brief vignette of American history illustrates that as leaders demonstrate individual abilities during challenging times, they are often called upon to step up to higher and more amorphous levels of organizational leadership. And the higher they go, the more they must account not just for their personal performance but also for the enduring capabilities and qualities of the organization they have come to represent. The uncomplicated ambition of individual success is now supplemented with the thorny and arduous aim of significance as an organization.

Today's world is in a high state of stress, and many individual leaders are distinguishing themselves in day-to-day transactions. Revolutions of many kinds are the order of the day. The questions we all must consider as we pass through this historic era of the largest scale of generational baton passing the world has ever seen are difficult despite their simplicity. Will these individual leaders scale their abilities and perspectives to include the highest levels of consideration for organizational significance? Or will they, in the struggle against this complexity, opt out by refusing advancement? Will they skirt the difficulty by allowing their individual leadership responsibilities to shrivel and lapse and think solely about large-scale organizational issues as mere economic or social abstractions? Or will they simply succumb to the seduction of obtaining as much personal power and financial gain as they can and leave the organization when their personal fortunes and interests are satisfied?

Individual leadership primarily concerns people and a call to action, while *organizational leadership* primarily concerns sustainable systems and generational legacies. Yet all organizational systems are comprised of people, and all people need some organizational system in order to contribute a lasting legacy. And so the endless cycle goes. Nearly all individuals, at some time, act as leaders—either through initiative or as a response to circumstance. Many people take on a series of different leadership roles throughout their lives that call upon their individual leadership abilities to a high degree and to a lesser degree require their organizational abilities. Fewer individuals (perhaps too few) take up the full mantle of individual and organizational leadership. Even with regard to Jim Collins's assertion of the numerous level-five leaders who have demonstrated their abilities but may never make a who's who list of famous commercial leaders, the evidence is grave. There are not nearly as many qualified candidates for organizational leadership positions who have integrated their individual leadership abilities with well-learned organizational leadership abilities.

Learning leadership with the goal of moving beyond individual success to reach organizational significance is a daunting ambition. We admire the leaders who make it and who truly encourage others to build their abilities and create a path for them to travel. Roughly half of the large companies in North America offer some form of training to assist in this process. Most countries of the European Union are similar in the level of their endeavors and in some ways have a more sophisticated posture. Japan and some Southeast Asian countries have growing appetites for leadership development rather than just managerial development. India's growth has created a huge need for development, and we anticipate leadership development systems will be a huge import business for that country in the near term. As with many other structural issues, the need for such systems in China is great, but the country is reluctant to absorb outside social constructs at any rapid pace, preferring to filter incoming ideas through their own worldviews in a deliberative manner.

Leadership development always begs the financial question of return on investment, yet this is not the only process that has ever come under fire. We could cite many senior leaders' admonitions that leadership development is imperative, and of course it pays off. We could cite those who cannot find a suitable method for determining whether or not the building of interpersonal skills such as leadership can be shown to pay off. We could also cite scholars like Henry Mintzberg, who basically inform us that attempting to measure the impact of leadership development is a fool's errand.[2] But rather than recount the numerous pros and cons, we will simply state our position with one example.

During the transition from the transactional era to the transformational era, when quality was becoming headline news for industrial companies, there were many people who wondered if gaining very high levels of quality cost more than it returned. The Japanese basically proved the case, but many people thought perhaps it was simply a localized effect that stemmed from Japanese social biases or if quality was something anyone could learn.

The CEO of Motorola at the time, Robert Galvin, son of the founder, put all his heart and mind into this issue. Quality became not just a goal but also a way of life at Motorola during a decade of difficult, demanding change. Motorola received the Malcolm Baldrige National Quality Award on its first attempt and in the first year of the award. Motorola workers everywhere were jubilant that their efforts were rewarded, and the company's Six Sigma process was admired and copied by many. The disputes over the cost of obtaining quality versus the returns of quality were settled, and for a time quality became the central business focus around the world.

In October 1990, Galvin spoke at the Economic Club in Chicago. Motorola's success had become world renowned, and interested businesspeople wanted to hear from a member of the founding family what his true thoughts and feelings were about how it all happened. Galvin titled his talk "The Heresies of Quality." He chose the word *heresy* because it means the act of challenging long-held truths, often leading to the discovery/creation of new truths. The thrust of his comments concerned the mental shifts required within quality programs and processes, particularly the cost of quality training. In that regard, he remarked:

> Here's where the leaders, and that's what we all are, have to engage in acts of faith. That things are doable that may not always at the instant be provable. I said, "Folks, I don't know how we're going to account for the ledgers, and the cash flows, through this thing called training. But it's never going to cost us a penny." The old truth was that training is overhead. And it's a cost. The new truth is that training is not a cost.[3]

And he went on to cite particulars concerning the effects of training and how once quality became a way of life, it would extend to suppliers, which in turn would create a major shift in relationships.

The story about leadership development is not different. In those cultures where leadership development has become a way of life, the returns significantly outweigh the costs. During the 1990s Galvin echoed Peter Drucker's thoughts about leadership development and began to announce that the limitation of quality in the course of the coming century was to be the quality of leadership. As a result, Motorola instituted more aggressive leadership development processes during this period.

The Motorola case is one of a thousand. Those who continue to try to measure the cost effectiveness of leadership development will likely lose the future to those who simply invest. That does not mean that due diligence of process capitulates to sentiment; leadership development processes should be as vigorously selected, deployed, and assessed as any other. It just seems futile to continue to delay leadership development until someone can show a predicable 20 percent return.

Individual leadership seems to be easier to master and more gratifying than gaining the more difficult abilities required of an organizational leader. Yet it is often those who can develop organizational abilities that help an organization sustain itself over time, and often the individuals who help this do not become famous or long remembered by many. Celebrity leadership of significant or interesting organizations often comes with the territory of taking up the mantle of leadership. Like other professions where significant success creates fanfare, status, and public review, being a celebrity isn't always what important leaders seek. It may come with the territory and in today's world is often another dimension that requires attention and sensitive action. It is also powerfully seductive.

More leaders are being required to move beyond the limits of their individual leadership abilities and gain more organizational leadership depth. It is hard work and organizations are not as skilled as they would like at helping individuals deal with the tensions this creates. Developing leaders is a demanding task for senior leaders everywhere and a task that likely should rank as a perpetual part of any organization's top five priorities.

Appendix

Forces That Shape Authenticity

IN THE chapter on Authenticity, we suggested four levels of personal investigation that could aid a leader's personal knowledge of self. The four levels were to gain understanding of behavior, natural talents, values, and motives.

In this appendix we have added a variety of thoughts and background references concerning how authenticity is developed. Each short section cites a variety of viewpoints that we hope will stimulate your interest in each area. We encourage you to use your own curiosity and investigative abilities to extend your knowledge.

Dialogical Processes

> The genesis of the human mind is in this sense not "monological," not something each accomplishes on his or her own, but dialogical.
> —Charles Taylor, *The Ethics of Authenticity*

Taylor argues that significant others help us see who we are in an exchange that is considered to be dialogical in nature. Even after they leave our lives, such as parental figures (regardless of their positive or negative influences), this dialogue continues, in varying degrees, throughout our lives.

> If I just listen to myself, I will be trapped in a circle. If you don't speak to me about what you see and suspect, then I won't know the direction in which I ought to go. And if I don't listen to my friends and neighbors, I'll be stuck in the labyrinth of what I think I want. —Thomas Moore, *Meditations: On the Monk Who Dwells in Daily Life*

Moore, a psychotherapist, writer, lecturer, and former monk of twelve years, in his slim volume concerning the melasmatic lifestyle of monks, even acknowledges that the practice of monkhood, the withdrawal and turning away from modern life, is not solely an exercise in monologue.

> It is not the isolated traumas of childhood that shape our future, but the quality of sustained relationships with important people.—George E. Vaillant, *Adaptation to Life*

Vaillant was the last of the psychologists to participate in the most famous longitudinal study perhaps ever conceived, known as the Grant Study. William T. Grant, dime store multimillionaire and philanthropist, financed the study, and the Grant Foundation continues its research into human behavior to this day. Grant wanted to increase understanding of how people who seem physically healthy develop over time. He felt too much emphasis had been placed on studying illness and maladaptive processes. The Grant Foundation has supported research by other famous individuals such as Dr. Benjamin Spock, Dr. Anna Freud, and Dr. Jane Goodall.

The Grant Study followed a group of more than two hundred Harvard graduates over fifty years of their lives. A variety of measures were used to assess these individuals' lives, including one-on-one interviews at various points. The results are impressive.

> Healthy leaders are passionate. At the same time they strongly believe in their ability to control (or at least affect) the events that impact their lives. They're able to take responsibility; they are not always scapegoating or blaming other people for what goes wrong. Healthy leaders don't easily lose control or resort to impulsive acts. They can work through their own anxiety and ambivalence. They are very talented in self-observation and self-analysis; the best leaders are highly motivated to spend time in self-reflection. They have the ability to deal with the disappointments of life. They can acknowledge their depression and work through it. Very importantly they have the capacity to establish and maintain relationships. Their lives are in balance, and they can play. They are creative and inventive and have the capacity to be nonconformist.—Manfred F. R. Kets de Vries, in Diane L. Koutu's "Putting Leaders on the Couch"

Kets de Vries, author of numerous leadership books and more than 150 scholarly research articles, also holds the Raoul de Vitry d'Avaucourt Chair of Human Resources Management at INSEAD, one of the best-known graduate schools of business in Europe.

He sees healthy leaders as engaging in strong relationships and also delving deep into their own minds and hearts for personal analysis and understanding. It is almost like they apply monkish investigations into their souls while living in the very real world.

Natural Talents

> To my mind, a human intellectual competence must entail a set of skills of problem solving—enabling the individual *to resolve genuine problems or difficulties* that he or she encounters and, when appropriate, to create an effective product—and must also entail the potential for *finding or creating problems*—thereby laying the groundwork for the acquisition of new knowledge.—Howard Gardner, *Frames of Mind: The Theory of Multiple Intelligences*

Gardner's conception of multiple intelligences, the original seven having expanded to nine, considers the neurobiological, as well as culturally sensitive, development of human ability. Note that his definition and explanation do not restrict themselves to mere neurological wiring patterns, but also to how the intelligence is developed over time in specific cultural settings.

> The real tragedy of life is not that each of us doesn't have enough strengths, it's that we fail to use the ones we have. —Marcus Buckingham and Donald O. Clifton, *Now, Discover Your Strengths*

They conclude that talents are naturally recurring patterns of thought, feeling, or behavior. This contrasts with knowledge, which consists of facts and lessons learned. Skills are essentially the steps of an activity.

Values

> We form our character in defining moments because we commit to irreversible courses of action that shape our personal and professional identities.—Joseph Badaracco, *Defining Moments: When Managers Must Choose Between Right and Right*

Badaracco is the John Shad Professor of Business Ethics at Harvard Business School. His most recent book, *Questions of Character: Illuminating the Heart of Leadership through Literature* (Boston: Harvard Business School Pres, 2006), explores questions concerning a leader's willingness to take responsibility, the flexibility of a moral code, how principles and pragmatism combine, and how character is judged.

> Leaders grow through mastering painful conflict during their developmental years.—Abraham Zaleznik, in Jay Conger's *Learning to Lead: The Art of Transforming Managers into Leaders*

Zaleznik is the Konosuke Matsushita Professor of Leadership, Emeritus at the Harvard Business School. A scholar, teacher, and psychoanalyst, he has studied leadership issues for more than fifty years. In the December 23, 2002, issue of *BusinessWeek*, he was interviewed about his thoughts on Dennis Kozlowski of the famed Tyco case. In the interview he speaks to how Kozlowski was able to gain supporters for his misdeeds: "So how does he enlist the people around him? He does it by force of personality. People identify with him, and through the seductive aspect of personality he takes over their conscience, their ability to distinguish right from wrong."

This inability to distinguish right from wrong is a fundamental hijacking of values that is perpetrated by a powerful, narcissistic personality.

> Those who are clear about their values and beliefs have laid the cornerstones for a firm ethical structure. People who have developed the skills to enact their beliefs possess the moral capacity to achieve good ends with good means. People who have faith in their abilities to execute effectively and consistently even under duress and challenge display moral fortitude. Moral structure, moral capacity, and moral fortitude combine to make a distinguished moral force in the world.—James M. Kouzes and Barry Z. Posner, *Credibility: How Leaders Gain It and Lose It, Why People Demand It*

Kouzes and Posner suggest that the first discipline of credibility is self-discovery. And they go on to suggest that beliefs, competence, and confidence are the content of character, or self. Two out of three of these involve interiors, with competence serving as an exterior.

Motivation

> An individual's motivational preference has real world consequences:
> it is demonstrably associated with vocational success and satisfaction.
> —Robert Hogan, *Motives, Values, and Intentions Manual*.

Hogan, developer of the famous series of Hogan personality assessments, is well-known leader in the area of leadership assessment. Extending the hard-won knowledge of early giants in the field, Hogan demonstrates that motives do indeed strongly influence leadership action.

> Suffice it to say, for now, that transferential reactions are a form of unconscious motivation. Many of our wishes and fantasies and fears are unconscious. But even lurking beneath the surface, they can motivate us.—Kets de Vries, *The Leadership Mystique*

Kets de Vries goes on in his work and in many of his books to speak on the psychology of leadership and the conscious and unconscious motives of leaders. He believes there is a rationale, a reason, for everything we do, even if it is unconscious. He also agrees, however, that people who are emotionally literate can conduct their own "deconstruction" or investigate these motives and bring more of the unconscious into the conscious realms.

Edward L. Deci and Richard Flaste have devoted their professional careers to self-determination theory. This is the study of motivation, autonomy, competence, self-esteem, and other matters as it relates to how humans actually wind up doing what they do. As the elements of intrinsic and extrinsic motivation was becoming clear in the research, they compiled much of the most important elements in their book *Why We Do What We Do: Understanding Self-Motivation* (New York: Penguin, 1996). This slim volume is a gem in the psychological world. Insights abound and the research is evocatively presented.

Deci's definition of intrinsic motivation is best described in his words: "I have always believed that the *experience* of intrinsic motivation is its own justification. Smelling the roses, being enthralled by how the pieces of a puzzle fit together, seeing the sunlight as it dances in the clouds, feeling the thrill of reaching a mountain summit: These are experiences that need yield nothing more to be fully justified. And one might go so far as to argue that a life devoid of such experiences is hardly a life at all" (46).

Being a scientist, however, he tested his biases and verified many important ideas that seem to be ignored often in the modern workplace. Among them are two worth noting here:

> If people do not believe that their behavior will lead to something they desire...they will not be motivated. The desired outcomes can be intrinsic satisfactions, or they can be extrinsic rewards, but people have to believe that some outcomes will accrue from their behavior or they will not be motivated to behave. (59)

> The urge to develop an integrated sense of self is thus a central feature of who we are as individuals, and the activity—both physical and mental—that is necessary for this natural developmental trajectory is intrinsically motivated. (80–81)

These findings dovetail with, as well as expand upon, the general thesis we are exploring in this book. Authenticity—this development of who we truly are and expanding our abilities—is not only a natural urge, but motivational factors play a big role in our successful self-development and in the integration of our true self in the entire scope of our life.

Resistances to Authenticity

The following thoughts refer to the darker side of self-development. We often resist developing greater insight and true character.

Categories of Resistance

Peter Koestenbaum, author of Leadership: *The Innerside of Greatness: A Philosophy for Leaders,* fled Germany prior to World War II with his parents and was raised in Venezuela. He taught at San Jose State University for thirty-four years, and his enduring contribution to leadership is a practical philosophy of development. He cites three types of resistance that people must overcome in their quest to gain greater authentic self-awareness. The first type is psychodynamic in nature, such as neuroses, dependencies, and childhood trauma. The second type of resistance is systemic, consisting of life views, or parts of the narratives we build up, such as a person's view on marriage, politics, society, business, or religion. The third type is the existential process of living through the anxiety of change.

Personality Disorders

A great deal of work concerning the massive destruction of highly competent, but personally flawed, leaders has been conducted. M. Scott Peck, a medical doctor most famous for the unexpected runaway success of his book *The Road Less Traveled: A New Psychology of Love, Traditional Values, and Spiritual Growth*, studied this issue in his equally powerful, even though lesser-known work *The People of the Lie: The Hope for Healing Human Evil*. He believes that a particular form of self-absorption, a type of narcissism, is the root cause of much of human evil. The various stories of the incomparable beauty of the Greek hero Narcissus are familiar to many. The convergence of the stories is simple. Narcissus fell in love with his own beauty, his own identity, and this self-absorption led to his destruction. In one version of the story he drowned in the pool where he stayed mesmerized by his reflection, the goddess Nemesis helping this along as a punishment of Narcissus's rejection of Echo. In another version he ends his life with his own sword due to the sorrow of his inability to love anyone but himself. Narcissism is named after this morality story and is linked to the word "narcotic" from the Greek root, *narke*, meaning numb.

Peck suggests that "malignant narcissism" is the variety of disorder that causes true human evil. Many infamous leaders from history may have suffered from this and caused suffering as a result.

Manfred Kets de Vries, in his book *Leaders, Fools, and Impostors*, also addresses the effects of narcissism on leaders. His examples include several well-known business leaders who, although they were tremendous in certain competency areas, eventually saw their leadership end in calamitous ways. He indicates that the lack of ability for self-reflection is one of the leading indicators of this form of narcissism. He also helps distinguish between the feelings of imposture, the feelings that we are unworthy, or are posing as something that we are not, from true narcissism. Most of us have feelings from time to time that we are truly not what others believe us to be, and we worry that if they really did know, things might be bad. The garden variety of this type of psychological episode is normal and actually helpful if it helps motivate true self-examination.

Notes

CHAPTER 1. FOUR LABORS

1. Ron Frieson quote, oral communication at BellSouth conference, January 30, 2006.

2. Urukagina and Sargon information from "Rise of the Human Race," http://www.emayzine.com/lectures/sumeria.htm. Additional sources for this material: http://www.answers.com/topic/urukagina; http://en.wikipedia.org/wiki/Urukagina; http://en.wikipedia.org/wiki/Sumeria; and http://en.wikipedia.org/wiki/Sargon_the_Great (all accessed on July 10, 2006).

3. Richard Kovacevich, "How Do We Picture Success?"

4. John T. Chambers, "Letter to Shareholders," Annual Report 2001.

5. John T. Chambers, quoted in "Cisco: Giving Back Is 'Good Business.'"

6. James MacGregor Burns, Leadership, 469.

7. Wilfred H. Drath, quoted in Joel Schettler, "Exclusive Research That Will Change the Way You Think about Leadership."

8. "Discovering New Drugs," from "How Things Work (in Science and Technology."

9. Katherine J. Klein and Steve W. J. Kozlowski, eds., *Multilevel Theory, Research, and Methods in Organizations*, 15.

10. Simon Mingay, John Mahoney, Mark P. McDonald, Michael A. Bell, "Redefining the Rules of IT Leadership."

11. Boyd Clarke and Ron Crossland, *The Leader's Voice*, 82.

12. Bill George, *Authentic Leadership*, 11.

13. Peter Georgescu, *The Source of Success*, 116.

14. Tom Peters, *Lessons in Leadership [Distinct... or Extinct?]* seminar.

15. Noel M. Tichy, *The Leadership Engine*, 80.

16. Manfred F. R. Kets de Vries, *The Leadership Mystique*, 265–67.

17. Gary Hamel, *Leading the Revolution*, 20–26.

18. James M. Kouzes and Barry Z. Posner, *The Leadership Challenge*, 109–90.

19. Virginia Postrel, *The Future and Its Enemies*, xvii.

20. C. K. Prahald and Venkat Ramaswamy, *The Future of Competition*, 2.

21. Michael Schrage, *Serious Play*.

22. Amy Kates, "(Re)Designing the HR Organization," 23.

23. David A. Nadler and Michael L. Tushman, *Competing by Design*, 52.

24. Ira Chaleff, *The Courageous Follower*, 31.

25. Tom Peters, *Lessons in Leadership* seminar, "Issue Y2K—the Great War for Talent! Legacy! (Or: Why Else Get Up in the Morning?)."

26. "Gallup Study: Feeling Good Matters in the Workplace."

27. Drucker, Peter. *Managing for the Future: The 1990s and Beyond*, 56.

28. Rakesh Khurana, *Chief Executive*, 19.

29. V. S. Ramachandran, *A Brief Tour of Human Consciousness*, 105.

30. John D. Sterman, "All Models Are Wrong," 501–31.

CHAPTER 2. AUTHENTICITY

1. The German expression is found in a variety of places. We accessed http://www.proverbium.eu/spr/srz1442.htm on July 11, 2006, as our source. The Afghan quote similarly was found on the same day at "Afghan Proverb Quotes," http://en.thinkexist.com/quotes/afghan_proverb/. The Chinese quotes were supplied by our colleagues in Bluepoint Leadership Development, Singapore, Ng Weng Jun and Chin Keong.

2. The charismatic former peasant cowherd Zhu Yuanzhang was taught in both Buddhist and Confucian traditions. His early life was replete with difficulty—from the hard work of peasant life, to living in a Buddhist monastery that eventually failed because of a lack of support, to (as legend suggests) having to beg for food. During this developmental period, however, he did learn to read and write, developed leadership skills while he was associated with the rebel group known as the Red Turban Movement, and adopted one of his learned advisers, Zhu Sheng's, leadership ideas: "Build high walls, stock up rations, and don't be too quick to call yourself a king."

Availing himself of that advice, Zhu Yuanzhang brokered alliances among many small rebel leaders throughout southern China and eventually headed an army large enough to ensure that the Han-led peasant revolt against the Mongolian-headed Yuan dynasty was successful. In 1368, after years of war and fending off a variety of national-level leaders, Zhu Yuanzhang declared himself emperor and set up a capital in Nanking. During his reign, he righted former wrongs by ensuring that peasants were treated more equitably by the government (via the institution of his "Yellow Records" and "Fish Scale Records" systems), buying back children whose starving parents had sold them as slaves, and releasing innocent people who had been imprisoned by the Mongols. During the Ming period, a large navy of sizable tonnage and a standing army of close to a million soldiers were created by the state for protection. Iron ore production increased, land use significantly increased and agriculture prospered, and many books were printed using moveable type. Web sites that might be useful for further background, accessed on July 1, 2006, are "Ming Dynasty," http://www.mnsu.edu/emuseum/prehistory/china/later_imperial_china/ming.html; "The Development of Porcelain in China," http://www.npm.gov.tw/exhbition/cpor2000/english/epor2000.htm; and "Dragon's Tomb," http://store.dragonstomb.com/index.html.

3. According to a news release on the ExxonMobil Web site ("Changes ExxonMobil Has Made to Prevent Another Accident Like Valdez"), since the Valdez incident, ExxonMobil has implemented the following:

- Modified tanker routes.
- Instituted drug and alcohol testing programs for safety-sensitive positions.
- Implemented more extensive periodic assessment of ExxonMobil vessels and facilities.

- Strengthened training programs for vessel captains and pilots.
- Applied new technology to improve vessel navigation and insure the integrity of oil containment systems.
- ExxonMobil is a founding member of every major oil spill response center worldwide.
- Created the award-winning oil spill dispersant, Corexit 9500.
- Deploy over 1,000 employees involved in oil spill response teams worldwide.
- Hold frequent, extensive oil spill drills at various ExxonMobil locations around the world.
- We have developed and applied new spill-detecting technology.

4. Kets de Vries, *Leadership Mystique,* 13–14.

5. John H. Humphreys and Walter O. Einstein, "Leadership and Temperament Congruence."

6. Ken Wilber, *Integral Psychology,* 38. Wilber, who is an influential figure in the integration movement that seeks to combine rationality with religion, psychology with spirit, science with intuition, and interiors with exteriors, goes on to speak on the benefits of conducting an archeological dig:

As usual, the more we go within, the more we go beyond. In the extraordinary archeology of Spirit, the deeper the level, the wider the embrace—the within that takes you beyond. Within the world of matter is the body, but the vital body goes beyond matter in so many ways: its feelings respond while rocks do not; its perceptions recognize a world while insentience sleeps; its emotions move a body while dirt awaits in silence. Likewise, the mind exists within the vital body, but the mind goes beyond the body in so many ways: while the body feels its own feelings, the cognition of the mind takes the role of others, and thus expands consciousness from egocentric to sociocentric to worldcentric; the mind knits together past and future, and thus rises above the impulsiveness of the body's instincts; while the mind conceives the world of what might be and what should be, the body slumbers in its naive present.

Likewise, looking deep within the mind, in the very most interior part of the self, when the mind becomes very, very quiet, and one listens very carefully, in that infinite Silence, the soul begins to whisper, and its feather-soft voice takes one far beyond what the mind could ever imagine, beyond anything rationality could possibly tolerate, beyond anything logic can endure. In its gentle whisperings, there are the faintest hints of infinite love, glimmers of a life that time forgot, flashes of a bliss of eternity breathe life into mortal time, where suffering and pain have forgotten how to pronounce their own names, this secret quiet intersection of time and the very timeless, an intersection called the soul.

In the archeology of the Self, deep within the personal lies the transpersonal, which takes you far beyond the personal; always within and beyond. Experienced previously only in peak experiences, or as a background intuition of immortality, wonder, and grace, the soul begins now to emerge more permanently in consciousness. Not yet infinite and all embracing, no longer merely personal and mortal, the soul is the great intermediate conveyor between pure Spirit and individual self. The soul can embrace the gross realm in nature mysticism, or it can plumb its own depths in deity mysticism. It can confer a postmortem meaning on all of life, and deliver grace to every corner of the psyche. It offers the beginning of an unshakable witnessing and equanimity in the midst of the slings and arrows of outrageous fortune, and breathes a tender mercy on all that it encounters. It is reached by a simple technique: turn left at mind, and go within. (106)

Those who find Wilber a bit too spiritually inclined and prefer a more scientific approach to the question of self might find V. S. Ramachandran's work of interest, such as this passage from his book *A Brief Tour of Human Consciousness:*

> What exactly is meant by the "self"? Its defining characteristics are five-fold. First of all, continuity: a sense of an unbroken thread running through the whole fabric of our experience with the accompanying feeling of past, present, and future. Second, and closely related, is the idea of unity or coherence of self. In spite of the diversity of sensory experiences, memories, beliefs and thoughts, we each experience ourselves as one person, as a unity.
>
> Third is a sense of embodiment or ownership—we feel ourselves anchored to our bodies. Fourth, a sense of agency, what we call free will, being in charge of our own actions and destinies. I can wiggle my finger but I can't wiggle my nose or your finger.
>
> Fifth, and most elusive of all, the self, almost by its very nature, is capable of reflection—of being aware of itself. A self that's unaware of itself is an oxymoron. (96)

7. While the period of 96 to 180 CE is historically identified as housing the five good Roman emperors—Nerva, Trajan, Hadrian, Antonius Pius, and Marcus Aurelius—that does not suggest that other emperors, such as Augustus, were not good. This "goodness" should also be placed in historical context, just as the behaviors of Urukagina and Sargon I should be. Life during these rulers' reigns was brutal and harsh, and although these leaders did bring a certain order and "civilization" to the period, in contemporary terms they may still be found wanting. However, life was also enhanced and some brutalities tamed to a degree as a result of various historical leaders' influence. The same could be said of much of modern society.

In Marcus Aurelius's case, his Stoic thought process has inspired generations of leaders to consider the content and context of leadership, as well as the need for continual self-examination. The following passage from his writings is an example of such ideas: "Nowhere can man find a quieter or more untroubled retreat than in his own soul; above all, he who possesses resources in himself, which he need only contemplate to secure immediate ease of mind—the ease that is but another word for well-ordered spirit. Avail yourself often, then, of this retirement, and so continually renew yourself." *Marcus Aurelius/Meditations,* trans. with an intro. by Maxwell Staniforth (Baltimore: Viking Penguin, 1964), 63.

8. Manfred F. R. Kets de Vries, *Leaders, Fools, and Impostors,* 179.

9. John W. Gardner, *On Leadership,* 8.

10. Laurence J. Peters, *Peter's Quotations,* 156.

11. Michelle Conlin, "She's Gotta Have It," 63.

12. Peter Ciampa, "How Leaders Move Up." 46–53.

13. Jim Collins, *Good to Great*.

14. Daniel Goleman, quoted in "Leading by Feel," 27–37.

15. Edwin Locke, quoted in Benedict Carey, "Sizing Up Emotions."

16. Antonio R. Damasio, *Descartes' Error*, xv.

17. "Definition of Asperger Syndrome," MedicineNet.com, http://www.medterms.com/script/main/art.asp?articlekey=9675, accessed December 7, 2006. The Web site also includes the following information:

> There is no specific course of treatment or cure for Asperger syndrome. Treatment, which is symptomatic and rehabilitation, may include both psychosocial and psychopharmacological interventions such as psychotherapy, parent education and training, behavioral modification, social skills training, educational interventions, and/or medications including psycho-stimulants, mood stabilizers, beta blockers, and tricyclic-type antidepressants.
>
> Children with Asperger syndrome have a better outlook than those with other forms of pervasive developmental disorders and are much more likely to grow up to be independently functioning adults. Nonetheless, in most cases, these individuals will continue to demonstrate, to some extent, subtle disturbances in social interactions. There is also an increased risk for development of psychosis (a mental disorder) and/or mood problems such as depression and anxiety in the later years.
>
> The syndrome is named for Hans Asperger who in 1944 published a paper that described a pattern of behavior in several young boys who had normal intelligence and language development but who had autistic-like behavior. Hans Asperger (1906–1980) was a pioneering pediatrician in Austria. He headed the play-pedagogic station at the university children's clinic in Vienna in 1932 and became director of the children's clinic in 1946. His special interest was in "psychically abnormal" children.

18. Steven Gutstein, quoted in "Leading by Feel," 27–37.

19. Jeremy W. Peters and Simon Romero, "Enron Founder Dies Before Sentencing."

20. "Kenneth Lay," obituary. The editors of *The Economist* were a little less forgiving of Lay even than some North American media, as evidenced by the following passage from their obituary.

> To the American public, Mr. Lay's greatest crime was to advise employees, as the firm crashed, to keep their Enron shares, or even to buy more, while he was selling his own to spin out a lavish lifestyle that he said he was unable to turn off "like a spigot." Many lost most of their savings as bankruptcy left their shares worthless. At his trial Mr. Lay tried to explain away his behaviour, saying that the sale was required to meet margin calls from his bankers, that Enron's lawyers had approved this, and that he was also buying Enron shares at the same time. But he did so without his famous charm, instead coming across as arrogant, prickly and, ultimately, unconvincing.
>
> To the end, Mr. Lay insisted that Enron was essentially a sound and highly profitable company, brought down by the equivalent of a run on the bank after the media reported relatively small thefts by the firm's chief financial officer, Andrew Fastow. Enron, Mr. Lay maintained, had introduced

important innovations in energy trading that benefited America's economy enormously (and which are now being practised by some of the world's leading investment banks). It had been accused, he once said, of being arrogant when it was simply "very innovative and very aggressive"—just like Drexel Burnham Lambert under Michael Milken, the "junk-bond king."

Mr. Milken was a friend of his, a man who, after serving time in jail, became one of America's leading philanthropists. Perhaps Mr. Lay hoped that his own story would have a similarly happy ending. But this was hardly a realistic hope. His chances of overturning conviction on appeal looked slim. He was much older than Mr. Milken when he was convicted. And he would have gone to jail for far longer, bearing in mind the new, tougher sentencing requirements.

Above all, as became clear only days before his death, apparently of a massive heart attack, the government had no intention of leaving him with any assets, to give away or not. He died as the face of America's turn-of-the-century corporate crime wave, and with none of the later compensations God allowed even to Job.

21. Romy Drucker, "The Devil Made Me Do It." Further analysis and contemplation of organizational ethical behavior is articulated by a number of authors. Numerous journals in North America and Europe allow academics, business professionals, and others to cite research findings, pose dilemmas, and debate the issues. The table of contents of just two of these publications point to the range of sensitive organizational authenticity issues. For example, at *Business Ethics: A European Review,* four recent intriguing articles listed were: Michael Luntley, *Ethics in the Face of Uncertainty: Judgment Not Rules*; Richard A. Spinello, *The Case Against Microsoft: An Ethics Perspective*; Robin Theobald, *Should the Payment of Bribes Overseas Be Made Illegal?* and Russell Sparkes, *Ethical Investment: Whose Ethics, Whose Investment?* And in the *Business and Professional Ethics Journal,* several articles in volumes 16 to 20 attract attention through some catchy titling: Vernon Kronenberg, *Beware of Geeks Bearing Gifts: Ethical Implications of Current Market Models of the Internet*; Paul A. Rahe, *Don Corleone, Multiculturalist*; and Howard Harris, *Is Love a Management Virtue?*

22. Simon Webley and Elise More, "Does Business Ethics Pay?"

23. Steve Yastrow, *Brand Harmony*, 6.

24. Richard Ettenson and Jonathan Knowles, "Merging the Brands and Branding the Merger," 40. These two researchers studied more than two hundred M&A deals from 1995 to 2005. Their research led them to identify ten basic strategies that were employed in such dealings. These ten strategies were streamlined to four basic messages that are communicated to customers, partners, investors, and employees. They are: (1) adopt the stronger brand identity; (2) adopt the best of both brands; (3) create a wholly new brand; and (4) make no brand changes. In all but the last strategy, an entire set of organizational authenticity questions emerge for all key stakeholders.

25. Napoleon Bonaparte Quotes, http://www.brainyquote.com/quotes/authors/n/napoleon_bonaparte.html, accessed August 29, 2006.

26. Manfred F. R. Kets de Vries, quoted in Diane L. Koutu, "Putting Leaders on the Couch," 70.

27. Napoleon Bonaparte Quotes.

Chapter 3. Navigation

1. Václav Havel, "The Power of the Powerless." In *The Struggle for Europe,* William Hitchcock concluded, "Havel's powerful essay 'The Power of the Powerless' argued that simply by 'living in truth'—by pointing out the falsehood and the lies that perpetuated the political system in Czechoslovakia—one could restore some humanity to oneself and one's neighbors" (302).

2. Edward L. Deci recalls his own experiences during his work in Bulgaria. In his book *Why We Do What We Do,* he wrote:

> For these workers, and for others in the Bulgarian system, outcomes such as enjoyment of their work, a satisfactory level of pay, and keeping their jobs were not contingent upon their work behavior, so there were no incentives for working. Certainly they would not have enjoyed their work in that cold, dirty room, running those machines, producing pieces of metal that may have had no purpose anyway (the storeroom was full of such things that were headed nowhere), so there would have been no intrinsic rewards for doing good work. Furthermore, the meager extrinsic rewards they received did not serve as motivators because they were not dependent on the quantity or quality of performance. And there were no threats of punishments for failing to work effectively (although, of course, the very fact of being there was itself punishing). Whey weren't they just fired? Because under the communist system the ethic was that everyone had the right to a job. Pay was dismal, but it was more or less guaranteed. The joke so often told by Bulgarians says it all: "They pretended to pay us and we pretended to work." (58)

3. Václav Havel, "New Year's Address to the Nation," Prague, January 1, 1991.

4. Ibid.

5. Howard Gardner, *Changing Minds,* 5. Gardner's book revolves around what he calls the seven R's of how to change minds. The definitions for these are:

- *Reason*—"A rational approach involves identifying of relevant factors, weighting each in turn, and making an overall assessment. Reason can involve sheer logic, the use of analogies, or the creation of taxonomies."

- *Research*—"Complementing the use of argument is the collection of relevant data. . . . But research need not be formal; it need only entail the identification of relevant cases and a judgment about whether they warrant a change of mind."

- *Resonance*—"A view, idea, or perspective resonates to the extent that it feels right to an individual, seems to fit the current situation, and convinces the person that further considerations are superfluous. . . . Resonance often comes about because one feels a 'relation' to a mind-changer, finds that person 'reliable,' or 'respects' that person—three additional 're' terms. . . . In most cases, rhetoric works best when it encompasses tight logic, draws on relevant research, and resonates with an audience."

- *Representational Redescriptions*—"A change of mind becomes convincing to the extent that it lends itself to representation in a number of different forms, with these forms reinforcing one another."

- *Resources and Rewards*—"Individuals are being rewarded for one course of behavior and thought rather than the other. Ultimately, however,

unless the new course of thought is concordant with the other criteria—
reason, resonance, research, for example—it is unlikely to last beyond the
provision of resources."

• *Real World Events*—"Sometimes an event occurs in the broader society
that affects many individuals, not just those who are contemplating a mind
change."

• *Resistances*—"Any effort to understand the changing of minds must
take into account the power of various resistances."

6. J. Gardner, *On Leadership*, 8.

7. Boris Groysberg, Andrew N. McLean, and Nitin Nohria, "Are Leaders Portable?"
The research indicates that general leadership and strategic skills are the most
portable, but the exact portfolio of these skills needs to match the needs of the new situation. In comparison after comparison of top GE talent that moved on to other companies, these authors concluded, "If managerial skill is transferable...what accounts
for the difference? Context" (94).

8. Joseph LeDoux, *The Emotional Brain*, 33.

9. Kathleen Hall Jamieson, *Eloquence in an Electronic Age*, 239. Jamieson continues her thoughts on mating the past and present, the old and the new, in terms of U.S.
national politics with the following:

> Those unschooled in the past readily confuse elegance with eloquence,
> conviction with cogency. Unable to recognize leadership when we see it, we
> careen from election to election searching for a candidate who compensates
> for the weaknesses of the president who has most recently failed us. After
> Nixon, an honest blue-jeans-wearing populist whose lack of Washington
> experience was considered a blessing; after Carter, competence and a confi-
> dence in the country; after Reagan, a command of detail and a strong man-
> agement style.
>
> From history we learn that what you see isn't always what you get. The
> past reveals that leadership often requires telling the citizenry truths it does
> not want to hear, that one test of the maturity of a people is a willingness to
> act on facts requiring sacrifice.
>
> We would conclude that Václav Havel invoked such truths about the
> past and present during his 1991 speech and appealed to the most mature
> levels, the deepest sense of personal competence and conviction, of a belea-
> guered people.

10. Cathy Gere, *The Tomb of Agamemnon*, 29.

11. J. Gardner, *On Leadership*, 191.

12. Nikos Mourkogiannis, *Purpose*, 18. Mourkogiannis is also a senior partner at
Panthea. He helped Roger Fisher (*Getting to Yes*) create the Harvard Law School
Center on Negotiations. His ideas about purpose range from classical to contemporary,
and his six key points on the concept of purpose are:

1. It is based on well-established moral ideas.

2. It advances both competitiveness and morality: it is in an area of overlap between the two.

3. It relates people to plans and it relates leaders to their colleagues.

4. It cannot be chosen, it has to be discovered, and this may take time and trial and error.

5. It is a matter of life or death—it is worth more money than anything else.

6. It is a paradox—it will boost profits only when pursued for its own sake. (18)

13. Michael Porter, "Now Is the Time to Rediscover Strategy."

14. David C. Wilson and Paula Jarzabkowski, "Thinking and Acting Strategically," 14–20. This entire issue was devoted to strategy, strategic thinking, and the newest ways scholars and practitioners consider strategy in context. Articles in the edition concerned crisis in strategy, strategy as practice, strategy as project, strategy after modernism, and strategy context with foresight. Other scholarly journals during this time period reflected similar increases in work published on strategy-related issues as the world economy turned upward.

15. Gary Hamel and C. K. Prahalad, *Competing for the Future.*

16. Dick Nettle, personal interview.

17. Peter Williamson and Ming Zeng, "Strategies for Competing in a Changed China," 85. Interestingly enough, these authors recommended what we consider to be five predictable, tried-and-true methods for taking advantage of what this new situation provides: (1) expand market coverage; (2) focus on dramatically lowering costs; (3) streamline distribution channels; (4) localize R&D; and (5) drive industry consolidation. What these five methods do, however, is help secure an advantage that conditions produced. They represent one portion of adaptive behavior—that is, taking advantage, securing territory, and making it more difficult to be uprooted. What these methods are *not* are strategies for ongoing adaptive behavior.

18. "Chinese Firm Buys IBM PC Business."

19. Bruce Einhorn, "Things Are Looking Lovelier for Lenovo."

20. Julian Birkinshaw and Cristina Gibson, "Building Ambidexterity into an Organization," 47. Birkinshaw and Gibson also cite several of the numerous early users of "ambidexterity" as a conceptual tool, such as Edward McDonough, Richard Leifer, Charles O'Reilly III, and Michael Tushman. In this article the authors outline what they believe are pathways to ambidexterity, which include:

- *Diagnose your organizational context:* Test the balance between performance management and social support.

- *Focus on a few levers, and employ them consistently:* Incentive compensation, risk management, and other levers have shown linkages to success. There is no magic in any special ones, but there is in consistently using ones that seem right for your organization.

- *Build understanding at all levels of the company:* The obvious nemesis of all organizational leaders—the farther away on the network from the leader, the more erosion to the message.

- *View contextual ambidexterity and structural ambidexterity as complements:* Conventional practice tends to separate alignment-oriented and adaptability-oriented activities, which solves some problems but creates others. Viewing them as complements rather than separate activities enhances the chances of reintegration.

• *View contextual ambidexterity initiatives as "driving leadership," not as being "leadership-driven"*: Fundamentally the coherent story must be conveyed by leaders at all levels of the organization.

21. Thomas A. Stewart, "Growth as a Process," 64.

22. Carl Sagan and Ann Druyan, *Shadows of Forgotten Ancestors*, 104.

23. Danielle Sacks, "Accidental Guru," 64. Of course this is a reframe from Anne Tyler's 1985 fabulous book, *The Accidental Tourist*, later recounted in a well-cast and well-played movie of the same title.

24. Malcolm Gladwell, *The Tipping Point*, 257. Gladwell's prominence as writer is mainly attributed to this work, although his skills as a writer were well known to a smaller audience for some period before publication of this book.

25. "Robert Greenberg," Reference for Business.

26. Alex Halperin, "Fancy Footwork at Brown and Skechers."

27. "Robert Greenberg," Reference for Business.

28. Additional information can be found under the title "Story of Nokia" at Nokia's Web site, but the basic story is as follows: "The history of Nokia goes back to 1865. That was when Fredrik Idestam built a wood pulp mill on the banks of the Tammerkoski rapids, in southern Finland. A few years later, he built a second mill by the Nokianvirta River—the place that gave Nokia its name."

Finnish Rubber Works merged with the wood pulp mill and Nokia was born. After the turn of the century and just before World War I, the Finnish Cable Works thrived as interest and demand for telegraph and telephone networks gripped the world. Shortly after World War II, the cable and rubber companies merged. Consolidation of the three operations took nearly another twenty years, but in 1967 the Nokia Group was fashioned.

The new Nokia turned their attention not just to transmission lines and the rubber needed to insulate those lines, but also to telephone switching. It continued to grow by means of the development of switching gear and acquisition.

Nokia developed Nordic Mobile Telephony, the world's first multinational cellular network, in 1981. This began the process that transformed Nokia into a worldwide brand. As GSM (global system for mobile communication) technology came on line and Nokia's prowess in mobile technology grew, the company shifted its emphasis to mobile technology. The 2100 cell phone series was mind-bogglingly successful—an original goal to sell five hundred thousand units turned into twenty million sold. Since 1990, Nokia has been divesting most of its interests outside its core telecommunications enterprise.

29. Henk W. Volberda, "Crisis in Strategy," 36.

30. Arthur M. Schlesinger Jr., "State of the 'Vision Thing'."

31. Arie De Geus, *The Living Company*, 11.

CHAPTER 4. ARCHITECTURE

1. Sources for coal tar, mauveine, Freidrich Englehorn, and William Henry Perkin come from a variety of Web sites, including the BASF Web site (all accessed

November 7, 2006). Vice rector Prof. Dr. Karlheinz Meier, speech honoring Professor Dr. Jürgen Strube, June 26, 2003, "Prof. Dr. Jürgen Strube New Honorary Senator of the University of Heidelberg," http://www.uni-heidelberg.de/press/news/press262_e.html; BASF Group, "1865–1901: The Birth of the Chemical Industry and the Era of Dyes," http://www.corporate.basf.com/en/ueberuns/profil/geschichte/1865-1901.htm?id=eR2yy9WI1bcp2L1; Henry Rzepa, "Mauveine: The First Industrial Organic Fine-Chemical," http://www.ch.ic.ac.uk/motm/perkin.html; and Wikipedia entry on Ludwigshafen am Rhein, http://en.wikipedia.org/wiki/Ludwigshafen

2. Meier speech.

3. Nadler and Tushman, *Competing by Design,* 6. Nadler and Tushman argue there are four factors in organizational architecture:

- *Purpose—*What is the organization's intended purpose?

- *Structural materials—*What "materials" do leaders-as-architects have available to use in constructing their organization?

- *Style—*What particular underlying motifs, needs, personality, or biases get incorporated into how the materials are used?

- *Collateral technology—*What technologies, systems, and modes of operating are not part of the main structural materials, but are necessary for the overall design to work?

4. Larry Bossidy and Ram Charan, *Confronting Reality,* 46.

5. Rosabeth Moss Kanter, "Innovation," 73. The various traps the venerable scholar offers for us to consider are as follows:

- Strategy Mistakes: Hurdles too high, scope too narrow.

- Process Mistakes: Controls too tight.

- Structure Mistakes: Connections too loose, separations too sharp.

- Skills Mistakes: Leadership too weak, communication too poor.

6. Jerry Hirshberg, *The Creative Priority,* 45.

7. Hirshberg quotes are from video-recorded proceedings of the conference in Ron Crossland's personal archive. This same story is recounted in Hirshberg's book, but hearing the author tell it added a certain depth and nuance that reading could not provide.

8. Annemieke van der Werff and Tamra Tammen, "Lost in Translation," *The Knowledge Lens,* no. 1, May 2005, 38.

9. Gordon MacKenzie, *Orbiting the Giant Hairball,* 17–20.

10. Personal interview notes, Julie Anixter interviewing Michael Schrage.

11. MacKenzie, *Orbiting the Giant Hairball,* 143–52.

12. Bruce Nussbaum and Rachel Tiplady, "Where MBAs Learn the Art of Blue-Skying."

13. Tom Kelley, *The Art of Innovation,* 121.

14. John W. Gardner, *Self-Renewal,* 63. Gardner also wrote about self-renewing organizations in his book *On Leadership.* In it he states five purposes for self-renewal.

1. To renew and reinterpret values that have been encrusted with

hypocrisy, corroded by cynicism or simply abandoned; and to generate new values when needed.

2. To liberate energies that have been imprisoned by outmoded procedures and habits of thought.

3. To reenergize forgotten goals or to generate new goals appropriate to new circumstances.

4. To achieve, through science or other modes of exploration, new understandings leading to new solutions.

5. To foster the release of human possibilities, through education and lifelong growth. (122)

15. Microsoft Corporation Annual Report 2006.

16. "Molecular Weight," 96.

17. Michael Lawton, "BASF Looks for Global Players."

18. Rob Hof, "Jeff Bezos' Risky Bet."

19. Laura McGinley, "Desperately Seeking Profitability."

20. Hof, "Jeff Bezos' Risky Bet."

CHAPTER 5. COMMUNITY

1. Aspen Institute mission statement.

2. James O'Toole's Web site (www.jamesotoole.com/bio.html) offers the following biography:

> O'Toole received his Doctorate in Social Anthropology from Oxford University, where he was a Rhodes Scholar. He served as a Special Assistant to Secretary of Health, Education and Welfare, Elliot Richardson, as Chairman of the Secretary's Task Force on Work in America, and as Director of Field Investigations for President Nixon's Commission on Campus Unrest. He won a Mitchell Prize for a paper on economic growth policy, has served on the prestigious Board of Editors of the *Encyclopaedia Britannica,* and was editor of *The American Oxonian* magazine.
>
> At USC he has held the University Associates' Chair of Management and served as Executive Director of the Leadership Institute. He has been editor of *New Management* magazine and Director of the Twenty-Year Forecast Project (where he interpreted social, political, and economic change for the top management of thirty of the largest US corporations). From 1994–97 O'Toole was Executive Vice President of the Aspen Institute. He also has served recently as Managing Director of the Booz Allen & Hamilton Strategic Leadership Center, and Chair of the Center's academic Board of Advisors.

3. James O'Toole, *Leading Change,* 5.

4. A listing of where Ensor's paintings can be found on the Internet is available at http://www.artcyclopedia.com/artists/ensor_james.html (accessed November 27, 2006). Ensor was an artistic trendsetter during a period of great innovation. While he studied history and religious painting and was also a draftsman, printmaker, and portrait painter, his efforts to push beyond the known to more innovative styles were stimu-

lated by his connection with *Les XX* ("The Twenty") a group that held an annual invitation-only exhibition of innovative art, including pieces from Ensor's fellow Belgian Fernand Knopff. Many of the group's invitees were among the French Impressionists and Fauveists, such as Claude Monet, Camille Pissarro, Georges Seurat, and Vincent van Gogh.

Ensor's work is considered by some to be a precursor to surrealist painting. Paul Klee mentions his admiration for Ensor in his diaries, and some of his techniques and innovations can be seen as adaptations in Marc Chagall's work.

As might be expected, Ensor and *Les XX* were vigorously attacked and rejected by the established art critic community, and *Les XX* eventually transformed into a new group, La Libre Esthétique. During the mid-1880s, a period of time just prior to painting his highly symbolic *Christ's Entry into Brussels in 1889*, Ensor suffered both an ulcer and his family's refusal to allow him to marry the woman he loved. He finished the painting during a depressive period following these events. It was listed in a *Les XX* catalog but was not shown publicly until 1929. The painting was considered vulgar, garish, and politically insulting, since some of Brussel's elected officials were depicted in a manner they felt was inappropriate. Ensor was so despondent at the time of this painting that he used some of his own features in constructing Christ's face. The painting remained in his possession all his life, and he occasionally made alterations to it.

Later in life, Ensor's abilities were recognized and appreciated—he was even created a baron. His most famous painting was hung in his hometown of Ostend, Belgium, for many years but was sold to the J. Paul Getty Museum in Los Angeles, where it now resides. In 1994 the Canadian band They Might Be Giants introduced a new generation to him with their song "Meet John Ensor" from the album *John Henry*. Patricia Gray Berman, a professor of art at Wellesley College, wrote a monograph about the painting that was published by the Getty museum in 2002.

5. O'Toole, *Leading Change*, 3.

6. Ibid., 4–6.

7. J. Gardner, *On Leadership*, 113.

8. Buckingham and Coffman. *Now, Discover Your Strengths*. New York: Free Press, 2001.

9. Donald L. Kanter and Philip H. Mirvis, *The Cynical Americans*.

10. Kets de Vries, *Leadership Mystique*, 94.

11. Tom Peters, "Issue Y2K," seminar slides, 2003. The following list of slides indicates which of Tom's numbered points we suggest dovetail with our engagement model in a very direct manner.

- Leaders cede control.
- Great Leaders on Snorting Steeds Are Important—but Great Talent Developers (Type I Leadership) are the Bedrock of Organizations that Perform Over the Long Haul.
- Great Leading = Great Mentoring.
- The Leader Is Rarely/Never the Best Performer.
- Leaders DO!
- Leaders Re-do.
- Leaders...DELIVER!

- Leaders Are . . . Optimists.
- Leaders FOCUS!
- Leaders...Set CLEAR DESIGN SPECS.
- Leaders Send V-E-R-Y Clear Signals About Design Specs!
- Leaders Trust in TRUST!
- Leaders Infuse the Dreaded-All Important "Evaluation Process" with CREDIBILITY!
- Leaders...Understand the Ultimate Power of RELATIONSHIPS.
- Leaders Are Natural EMPOWERMENT FREAKS!
- Leaders Have to Deliver, So They Worry About "Throwing the Baby Out with the Bathwater."
- Leaders...HONOR THE USURPERS.
- Leaders Honor Mistakes & Create "Blame-free 'Cultures.'"
- When It Comes to TALENT...Leaders Always Swing for the Fences!
- Leaders Don't Create "Followers": THEY CREATE LEADERS!
- Leaders Pursue Poets!
- Leaders Know: ENTHUSIASM BEGETS ENTHUSIASM!
- Leaders Focus on the SOFT STUFF!
- Leaders LOVE "POLITICS."
- Leaders Give...RESPECT!
- Leaders Say "Thank You."
- Leaders LAUGH!
- Leaders Don't Scapegoat / Allow Scapegoating.

12. Max DePree, *Leadership Is an Art*, 27.

13. Rich Anderson, "The United States Army in World War II."

14. Bernard M. Bass, ed., *Bass & Stogdill's Handbook of Leadership*, 379.

15. We suggest reading James M. Kouzes and Barry Z. Posner's *Encouraging the Heart* as a practical primer on how to use rewards inside of an appreciative mind-set.

16. Steven Berglas, "How to Keep A Players Productive," 105–06.

17. Muhammad Yunus interview.

18. "Bangalore Boom."

19. "The Battle for Brainpower," 9.

20. Thomas L. Friedman, *The World Is Flat*, 5.

21. "Battle for Brainpower."

22. R. Wang and Mervyn T. Adrian, "Battle Royale of Software Ecosystems."

23. Jonathan Head, "Japan Sounds Alarm on Birth Rate."

24. Elisabeth Niejahr, *Altenrepublik*.

25. *Chief Executive*, September 2003, survey data.

26. DNM Strategies and BusinessWeek, "Beyond the Hype."

27. Paul Bernthal and Richard Wellins, "Trends in Leader Development and Succession," 33. What is fascinating to us about this particular study is the list of reasons why internal leaders fail. It matches our four labors of leaders in a significant way. The following two charts are from this same report.

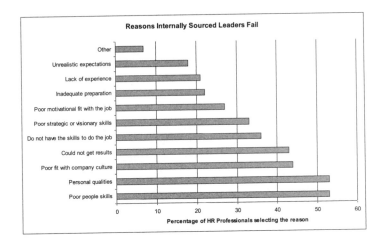

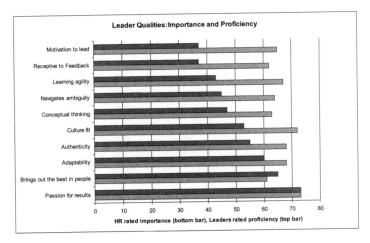

28. *Fortune* 151, no. 4 (February 21, 2005), http://money.cnn.com/magazines/fortune/fortune_archive/2005/02/21/toc.html.

29. Fernandez-Araoz, Claudio, "Getting the Right People at the Top," Sloan Management Review, Summer, 2005, 68.

30. Harris Interactive, www.harrisinteractive.com/wirthlin (accessed August 27, 2005).

31. Jay A. Conger and Robert M. Fulmer, "Developing Your Leadership Pipeline," 81.

32. Scott W. Spreier, Mary H. Fontaine, and Ruth L. Malloy, "Leadership Run Amok," 72.

33. Vanessa Urch Druskat and Jane V. Wheeler, "How To Lead a Self-Managing Team," 65–71. In addition to reviewing the literature on self-managed teams over all three eras (transactional, transformational, and transcultural), these authors conducted their own independent study as well. Their findings suggest that leaders who oversee self-managing teams run smack into the tensions of individual and organizational leadership at a higher frequency than other managers. The four key competencies they found for the successful leader in this case were relating, scouting, persuading, and empowering.

34. Rakesh Khurana, *Searching for a Corporate Savior*, 112.

35. Jeffrey Cohn and Rakesh Khurana, "How to Succeed at CEO Succession," 10–16, 24. Available at http://www.refresher.com/!jcrksuccession.html. 36. Nanette Byrnes, "Star Search," 69.

36. Don Tapscott and Anthony D. Williams, *Wikinomics*, .12

CHAPTER 6. CASE STUDIES

1. The Andrew Higgins case study material was largely created through the study of Stephen Ambrose's book *D-Day, June 6, 1944: The Climactic Battle of World War II* (New York: Simon and Schuster, 1994) and Jerry Strahan's *Andrew Jackson Higgins and the Boats That Won World War II* (Baton Rouge: Louisiana State University Press, 1994). The following Web sites were accessed during the summer of 2005: Hugh Sidey, "The Homefront" (June 24, 2001), http://www.time.com/time/archive/preview/0,10987,1101940613-164555,00.html, and http://www.higginsboat.org/html/news/news9912.html.

2. The Mary Kay Ash story was developed primarily from the Mary Kay Ash Web site (www.marykay.com) and the following additional Web sites, all accessed in the summer of 2005: Janet Mace Valenza, "Mineral-Water Springs and Wells," Handbook of Texas Online, http://www.tsha.utexas.edu/handbook/online/articles/view/MM/sbm11.html; Keli Flynn, "Mary Kay Cosmetics," Handbook of Texas Online, http://www.tsha.utexas.edu/handbook/online/articles/view/MM/dhm1.html; Leo Kee Chye, "Mary Kay Ash," Chutzpah series, Stoneforest.org, March 13, 2005, http://www.stoneforest.org/chutzpah/mary_kay_ash.html; "Mary Kay Ash: 1915–2001," Cool Texas Women, University of Texas Women's Resource Center, http://studentorgs.utexas.edu/wrc/cool.htm; http://www.marykay.com/; Chris Pearson, "Jury Awards $11.2M in Mary Kay Suit," Legal News Watch, January 21, 2003 http://www.legalnewswatch.com/news_103.html; Susannah Patton, "Lip Service," CIO, Web Business 50 Awards, December 1, 2001, http://www.cio.com/archive/120101/rule_marykay.html.

3. The Akio Morita story was developed from the following issues of *The Economist*: October 7, 1999; February 24, 2000; October 30, 2003; March 10, 2005. Three other articles were also reviewed: the March 13 edition of the *Sunday Independent*; Marilyn Mand, "Challenge of Entrepreneurship in a Developed Economy: The Problematic Case of Japan," *Journal of Developmental Entrepreneurship*, December 2003; and Nathan Layne, "Sony to Cut 10,000 Jobs," *PC Magazine*, September 2005. The following Web-based sources were also reviewed during the

summer of 2005: Keniche Ohmehe, "Builders and Titans," The Time 100: Akio Morita, Time.com., http://www.time.com/time/time100/builder/profile/morita3.html; "Akio Morita," Wikipedia, http://en.wikipedia.org/wiki/Akio_Morita; and "Postwar Japan: The U.S. Shogunate," http://www.emayzine.com/lectures/JAPANPW.html.

Chapter 7. Success to Significance

1. Washington background material was sourced from the following Web sites, accessed December 21, 2006: http://www.mountvernon.org/learn/meet_george/index.cfm/ss/21/;http://www.americanrevwar.homestead.com/files/GWASH.HTM; http://www.whitehouse.gov/history/presidents/gw1.html.

2. Henry Mintzberg,

3. Robert W. Galvin, "The Heresies of Quality."

Bibliography

Anderson, Rich. "The United States Army in World War II." Military History Online. http://www.militaryhistoryonline.com/wwii/usarmy/manpower.aspx (accessed December 13, 2006).

Aspen Institute mission statement. http://www.aspeninstitute.org/site/c.huLWJeMRKpH/b.493947/k.7AC3/About_the_Aspen_Institute.htm.

"Bangalore Boom." Red Herring, Inc. January 21, 2004. http://www.career-graph.com/gen_articles/bangaloreboom/index.shtml (accessed December 1, 2006).

Bass, Bernard M., ed. *Bass & Stogdill's Handbook of Leadership: Theory, Research, and Managerial Applications.* New York: Free Press, 1990.

"The Battle for Brainpower: A Survey of Talent." *The Economist* (October 7, 2006).

Berglas, Steven. "How to Keep A Players Productive." *Harvard Business Review* (September 2006). Available at http://custom.hbsp.com/b01/en/implicit/viewFileNavBeanImplicit.jhtml?_requestid=23288.

Bernthal, Paul, and Richard Wellins. "Trends in Leader Development and Succession." *Human Resource Planning* 29, no. 2 (2006). 0Available at http://www.questia.com/PM.qst;jsessionid=F6CQ9JthVdvWD0fmT86Yfjd2XfdkvGSnXG4yTLxTHFT NhSRmh9hm!-1316611484!954715203?a=o&d=5016028893.

Birkinshaw, Julian, and Cristina Gibson. "Building Ambidexterity into an Organization." *MIT Sloan Management Review* 45, no. 4 (Summer 2004). Available at http://sloanreview.mit.edu/smr/issue/2004/summer/08/.

Bossidy, Larry, and Ram Charan. *Confronting Reality: Doing What Matters to Make Things Right.* New York: Crown Business, 2004.

Buckingham, M., and C. Coffman. *Now, Discover Your Strengths.* New York: Free Press, 2001.

Burns, James MacGregor. *Leadership.* New York: Harper & Row, 1978.

Business Ethics: A European Review. http://www.blackwellpublishing.com/journal.asp?ref=0962-8770 (accessed July 21, 2006).

Business and Professional Ethics Journal. http://www.ethics.ufl.edu/BPEJContents_Volumes_16-20/contents_volumes_16-20.html (accessed July 21, 2006).

Byrnes, Nanette. "Star Search: How to Recruit, Train, and Hang On to Great People—What Works, What Doesn't." *BusinessWeek* (October 10, 2005).

Carey, Benedict. "Sizing up Emotions: The Value of Emotional Intelligence Tests, Widely Used by Employers, Is Being Questioned." *Los Angeles Times,* March 15, 2004, F-1.

Chaleff, Ira. *The Courageous Follower: Standing Up to and For Our Leaders,* 2nd ed. San Francisco: Berrett-Koehler, 2003.

Chambers, John T. "Letter to Shareholders," Cisco Annual Report 2001. Available at http://www.cisco.com/web/about/ac49/ac20/ac19/ar2001/letters/index.html.

Quoted in "Cisco: Giving Back Is 'Good Business.'" *BusinessWeek,* August 11, 2005. Available at http://www.businessweek.com/technology/content/aug2005/tc20050811_6009_tc057.htm.

"Changes ExxonMobil Has Made to Prevent Another Accident Like Valdez." News release. http://www.exxonmobil.com/corporate/Newsroom/NewsReleases/Corp_NR_Changes.asp (accessed July 1, 2006).

"Chinese Firm Buys IBM PC Business." BBC news. December 8, 2004. http://news.bbc.co.uk/2/hi/business/4077579.stm (accessed August 28, 2006).

Ciampa, Peter. "How Leaders Move Up." *Harvard Business Review* 83, no. 1 (January 2005). Special issue.

Clarke, Boyd, and Ron Crossland. *The Leader's Voice: How Your Communication Can Inspire Action and Get Results!* New York: Select Books, 2002.

Cohn, Jeffrey, and Rakesh Khurana. "How to Succeed at CEO Succession: Aligning Strategy and Succession." *Directorship* 29, no. 5 (May 2003). Available at http://www.refresher.com/!jcrksuccession.html.

Collins, Jim. *Good to Great: Why Some Companies Make the Leap—and Others Don't.* New York: HarperBusiness, 2001.

Conger, Jay A., and Robert M. Fulmer. "Developing Your Leadership Pipeline." *Harvard Business Review* 81, no. 12 (December 2003).

Conlin, Michelle. "She's Gotta Have It." *BusinessWeek* (July 22, 2002).

Damasio, Antonio R. *Descartes' Error: Emotion, Reason, and the Human Brain.* New York: Putnam, 1994.

Deci, Edward L. *Why We Do What We Do: The Dynamics of Personal Autonomy.* New York: Putnam's Sons, 1995.

De Geus, Arie. *The Living Company: Habits for Survival in a Turbulent Business Environment.* Boston: Harvard Business School Press, 1997.

DePree, Max. *Leadership Is an Art.* New York: Dell Publishing, 1990.

"Discovering New Drugs." From "How Things Work (in Science and Technology." *Research/Penn State* 20, no. 2 (May 1999). Available at Penn State Online Research, http://www.rps.psu.edu/howthings/newdrugs.html.

Drucker, Romy. "The Devil Made Me Do It." Up Front. Ethics section. *BusinessWeek Online.* July 24, 2006. http://www.businessweek.com/magazine/content/06_30/c3994003.htm?chan=search.

Druskat, Vanessa Urch, and Jane V. Wheeler. "How To Lead a Self-Managing Team." *MIT Sloan Management Review* 45, no. 4 (Summer 2004).

Einhorn, Bruce. "Things Are Looking Lovelier for Lenovo." *BusinessWeek Online.* August 4, 2006. http://www.businessweek.com/globalbiz/content/aug2006/gb20060804_701548.htm?chan=top+news_top+news.

Ettenson, Richard, and Jonathan Knowles. "Merging the Brands and Branding the Merger." *MIT Sloan Management Review* 47, no. 4 (Summer 2006).

Friedman, Thomas L. *The World Is Flat: A Brief History of the Twenty-first Century.* New York: Farrar, Straus, and Giroux, 2006.

"Gallup Study: Feeling Good Matters in the Workplace." *Gallup Management Journal.* January 12, 2006. http://gmj.gallup.com/content/20770/Gallup-Study-Feeling-Good-Matters-in-the.aspx.

Galvin, Robert W. "The Heresies of Quality." Speech given at the Economic Club of Chicago, October 25, 1990. Available at http://www.econclubchi.org/History/Excerpts_RobertWGalvin.pdf (accessed December 21, 2006).

Gardner, Howard. *Changing Minds: The Art and Science of Changing Our Own and Other People's Minds.* Boston: Harvard Business School Press, 2004.

Gardner, John W. *On Leadership*. New York: Free Press, 1989.

Self-Renewal: The Individual and the Innovative Society, rev. ed. New York: Norton, 1981.

George, Bill. *Authentic Leadership: Rediscovering the Secrets to Creating Lasting Value*. San Francisco: Jossey-Bass, 2003.

Georgescu, Peter. *The Source of Success: Five Enduring Principles at the Heart of Real Leadership*. San Francisco: Jossey-Bass, 2005.

Gere, Cathy. *The Tomb of Agamemnon*. Cambridge, MA: Harvard University Press, 2006.

Gladwell, Malcolm. *The Tipping Point: How Little Things Can Make a Big Difference*. Boston: Little, Brown, 2000.

Groysberg, Boris, Andrew N. McLean, and Nitin Nohria. "Are Leaders Portable?" *Harvard Business Review* 84, no. 5 (May 2006).

Halperin, Alex. "Fancy Footwork at Brown and Skechers." *BusinessWeek Online*. February 17, 2006. http://www.businessweek.com/investor/content/feb2006/pi20060217_558312.htm?chan=search (accessed March 3, 2006).

Hamel, Gary. *Leading the Revolution*. Boston: Harvard Business School Press, 2000.

Gary Hamel and C. K. Prahalad. *Competing for the Future*. Boston: Harvard Business School Press, 1994.

Havel, Václav. "The Power of the Powerless." October 1978. http://www.vaclavhavel.cz/showtrans.php?cat=clanky&val=72_aj_clanky.html&typ=HTML (accessed July 27, 2006).

"New Year's Address to the Nation." Prague, January 1, 1991. http://old.hrad.cz/president/Havel/speeches/index_uk.html (accessed July 27, 2006).

Head, Jonathan. "Japan Sounds Alarm on Birth Rate." *BBC News*. December 3, 2004. http://news.bbc.co.uk/2/hi/asia-pacific/4065647.stm (accessed December 1, 2006).

Hirshberg, Jerry. *The Creative Priority: Driving Innovative Business in the Real World*. New York: HarperBusiness, 1998.

Hitchcock, William. *The Struggle for Europe: The Turbulent History of a Divided Continent, 1945<N>2002*. New York: Doubleday, 2003.

Hof, Rob. "Jeff Bezos' Risky Bet." *BusinessWeek Online*. November 13, 2006. Available at http://www.businessweek.com/magazine/content/06_46/b4009001.htm.

Humphreys, John H., and Walter O. Einstein. "Leadership and Temperament Congruence: Extending the Expectancy Model of Work Motivation." *Journal of Leadership and Organizational Studies* (March 22, 2004).

Jamieson, Kathleen Hall. *Eloquence in an Electronic Age: The Transformation of Political Speechmaking*. New York: Oxford University Press, 1988.

Kanter, Donald L., and Philip H. Mirvis. *The Cynical Americans: Living and Working in an Age of Discontent and Disillusion*. San Francisco: Jossey-Bass, 1989.

Kanter, Rosabeth Moss. "Innovation: The Classic Traps." *Harvard Business Review* 84, no. 11 (November 2006).

Kates, Amy. "(Re)Designing the HR Organization." *Human Resource Planning* 29, no. 2 (June 2006).

Kelley, Tom. *The Art of Innovation: Lessons in Creativity from IDEO, America's Leading Design Firm*. New York: Currency/Doubleday, 2001.

"Kenneth Lay." Obituary. *The Economist*, July 6, 2006. Available at http://www.economist.com/obituary/displaystory.cfm?story_id=EL_STQTNDT.

Kets de Vries, Manfred F. R. *The Leadership Mystique: Leading Behavior in the Human Enterprise.* New York: Prentice Hall/Financial Times, 2001.

Leaders, Fools, and Impostors: Essays on the Psychology of Leadership. San Francisco: Jossey-Bass, 1993.

Khurana, Rakesh. *Chief Executive.* October 2003.

Searching for a Corporate Savior: The Irrational Quest for Charismatic CEOs. Princeton, NJ: Princeton University Press, 2002.

Klein, Katherine J., and Steve W. J. Kozlowski, eds. *Multilevel Theory, Research, and Methods in Organizations: Foundations, Extensions, and New Directions.* San Francisco: Jossey-Bass, 2000.

Koestenbaum, Peter. *Leadership: The Innerside of Greatness: A Philosophy for Leaders.* San Francisco: Jossey-Bass, 1991.

Koutu, Diane L. "Putting Leaders on the Couch: A Conversation with Manfred F. R. Kets de Vries." *Harvard Business Review* 82, no. 1 (January 2004).

Kouzes, James M., and Barry Z. Posner. *The Leadership Challenge,* 3rd ed. San Francisco: Jossey-Bass, 2002.

Encouraging the Heart: A Leader's Guide to Rewarding and Recognizing Others. San Francisco: Jossey-Bass, 2003.

Kovacevich, Richard. "How Do We Picture Success?" Wells Fargo Web site. https://www.wellsfargo.com/invest_relations/vision_values/3 (accessed July 10, 2006).

Lawton, Michael. "BASF Looks for Global Players." *HERE: The Alfa Laval International Customer Magazine.* May 22, 2000. http://here.alfalaval.com/?pageID=3&articleID=32&keyTechnologyID=3 (online edition accessed on November 20, 2006).

"Leading by Feel." *Harvard Business Review* 82, no. 1 (January 2004).

LeDoux, Joseph. *The Emotional Brain: The Mysterious Underpinnings of Emotional Life.* New York: Simon and Schuster, 1998.

MacKenzie, Gordon. *Orbiting the Giant Hairball: A Corporate Fool's Guide to Surviving with Grace.* Shawnee Mission, KS: OpusPocus Publications, 1996.

McGinley, Laura. "Desperately Seeking Profitability," Princeton Packet Online. November 9, 2000. http://www.pacpubserver.com/new/business/11-9-00/bezos.html (accessed March 5, 2007).

Microsoft Corporation Annual Report 2006, http://www.microsoft.com/msft/reports/ar06/staticversion/10k_fr_dis.html (accessed on November 30, 2006).

Mingay, Simon, John Mahoney, Mark P. McDonald, and Michael A. Bell. "Redefining the Rules of IT Leadership." Gartner Research, July 1, 2004. Available at http://www.gartner.com/DisplayDocument?doc_cd=121657.

Mintzberg, Henry.

"Molecular Weight: BASF and the Chemical Industry (Using the Verbund Method for Planning Business Sites)," *The Economist* (November 2, 2006).

Mourkogiannis, Nikos. *Purpose: The Starting Point of Great Companies.* New York: Palgrave, 2006.

Nadler, David A., and Michael L. Tushman. *Competing by Design: The Power of Organizational Architecture.* New York: Oxford University Press, 1997.

Niejahr, Elisabeth. *Altenrepublik* [Republic of the Old]. Frankfurt/Main: S. Fischer Verlag, 2004.

Nussbaum, Bruce, and Rachel Tiplady. "Where MBAs Learn the Art of Blue-Skying." *BusinessWeek*, April 18, 2005. Available at http://www.businessweek.com/magazine/content/05_16/b3929040_mz011.htm.

O'Toole, James. *Leading Change: The Argument for Values-Based Leadership.* San Francisco: Jossey-Bass, 1996.

Peck, M. Scott. *The Road Less Traveled: A New Psychology of Love, Traditional Values, and Spiritual Growth.* New York: Simon and Schuster, 1978.

The People of the Lie: The Hope for Healing Human Evil. New York: Simon and Schuster, 1983.

Peters, Jeremy W., and Simon Romero. "Enron Founder Dies Before Sentencing." *New York Times,* July 5, 2006. Online edition, http://www.nytimes.com/2006/07/05/business/05cnd-lay.html?ex=1167710400&en=bf71715b27ec1381&ei=5087&excamp=GGBUkenlay (accessed July 20, 2006).

Peters, Laurence J. *Peter's Quotations: Ideas for Our Time.* New York: Quill/Morrow, 1992.

Peters, Tom. *Lessons in Leadership [Distinct...or Extinct?].* Seminar slides, 2004.

Lessons in Leadership. Seminar. "Issue Y2K—the Great War for Talent! Legacy! (Or: Why Else Get Up in the Morning?)" Slide series. October 15, 2003.

Porter, Michael. "Now Is the Time to Rediscover Strategy." *Wall Street Journal,* November 2001. Also published in *European Business Forum,* vol. 8. Available at Many Worlds: Thought Leadership for Business, http://www.manyworlds.com/default.aspx?from=/exploreCO.aspx&coid=CO327021083398 (accessed March 5, 2007).

Postrel, Virginia. *The Future and Its Enemies: The Growing Conflict over Creativity, Enterprise, and Progress.* New York: Free Press, 1998.

Prahald, C. K., and Venkat Ramaswamy. *The Future of Competition: Co-Creating Unique Value with Customers.* Boston: Harvard Business School Publication, 2004.

Ramachandran, V. S. *A Brief Tour of Human Consciousness: From Imposter Poodles to Purple Numbers.* New York: Pi Press, 2004.

"Robert Greenberg," Reference for Business. Business Biographies. http://www.referenceforbusiness.com/biography/F-L/Greenberg-Robert-1940.html (accessed August 30, 2006).

Sacks, Danielle. "Accidental Guru." *Fast Company,* no. 90 (January 2005). Available at http://www.fastcompany.com/magazine/90/open_gladwell.html.

Sagan, Carl, and Ann Druyan. *Shadows of Forgotten Ancestors: A Search for Who We Are.* New York: Ballantine Books, 1993.

Schettler, Joel. "Exclusive Research That Will Change the Way You Think about Leadership." Center for Creative Leadership. http://joelschettler.com/images/uploads/306_CCL.pdf.

Schlesinger, Arthur M., Jr. "State of the 'Vision Thing'." *Los Angeles Times,* January 21, 2004.

Schrage, Michael. *Serious Play: How the World's Best Companies Simulate to Innovate.* Boston: Harvard Business School Press, 2000.

Spreier, Scott W., Mary H. Fontaine, and Ruth L. Malloy. "Leadership Run Amok: The Destructive Potential of Overachievers." *Harvard Business Review* (November 2006).

Sterman, John D. "All Models Are Wrong: Reflections on Becoming a Systems Scientist." *Systems Dynamics Review* 18, no. 4 (Winter 2002).

Stewart, Thomas A. "Growth as a Process: The HBR Interview." Interview with Jeffery Immelt. *Harvard Business Review* 84, no. 6 (June 2006). Available at http://www.ge.com/files/usa/company/investor/downloads/harvard_business_review_ge.pdf.

"Story of Nokia." Nokia corporate Web site. http://www.nokia.com/A4303001 (accessed March 4, 2007).

Tapscott, Don, and Anthony D. Williams. *Wikinomics: How Mass Collaboration Changes Everything*. New York: Portfolio, 2007.

Tichy, Noel M. *The Leadership Engine: How Winning Companies Build Leaders at Every Level*. New York: Harper Business, 1997.

van der Werff, Annemieke, and Tamra Tammen. "Lost in Translation." *The Knowledge Lens*, no. 1 (May 2005).

Volberda, Henk W. "Crisis in Strategy: Fragmentation, Integration or Synthesis." *European Management Review* 1, no. 1 (2004).

Wang, R., and Mervyn T. Adrian. "Battle Royale of Software Ecosystems: SIs Too Can Lead the Way." NASSCOM Newsline, no. 61 (November 2006). http://www.nasscom.in/Nasscom/templates/NormalPage.aspx?id=50557 (accessed December 1, 2006).

Webley, Simon, and Elise More. "Does Business Ethics Pay?" Institute of Business Ethics paper. April 2003.

Wilber, Ken. *Integral Psychology: Consciousness, Spirit, Psychology, Therapy*. Boston: Shambhala, 2000.

Williamson, Peter, and Ming Zeng. "Strategies for Competing in a Changed China." *MIT Sloan Management Review* 45, no. 4 (Summer 2004). Available at http://sloanreview.mit.edu/smr/issue/2004/summer/13/.

Wilson, David C., and Paula Jarzabkowski. "Thinking and Acting Strategically: New Challenges for Interrogating Strategy." *European Management Review* 1 (Spring 2004).

Yastrow, Steve. *Brand Harmony: Achieving Dynamic Results by Orchestrating Your Customer's Total Experience*. New York: Tom Peters Company Press, 2003.

Yunus, Muhammad. Interview. Nobel Prize Web site. http://nobelprize.org/nobel_prizes/peace/laureates/2006/yunus-interview.html (accessed November 27, 2006).

Index